Stories My Father Told Me

From Warsaw, Moscow, Algeria, Siberia, Kazakhstan, Dominican Republic

Dvora Treisman

Dedication

For my father

In memory of my father and mother and the
family I never met:
Abram, Sonia, Ignacy, Dora, Irena, Estusia, and
Kuba

Contents

Preface

Towards the end of his life, my father, Rafał Feliks Buszejkin, wrote a personal memoir, the story of his life. He meant it to be for me so that I would know about my background and the family I never met. He worked on it for several years, writing it in English, and he must have written the first draft by hand because whoever typed it didn't know Russian or Polish so there were countless misspellings of the names of people and places. I don't know Russian or Polish either, and so it took me more time than it should have to finally figure out that many of those t's were actually l's.

I read his manuscript many years ago, even made some notes in the margins and some highlights in orange and pink. Then I put it on a shelf. It was only recently, while looking for a specific and very basic piece of information about my father, that I dusted it off, started to look, and couldn't stop reading.

There were actually three drafts. They all began at the same time and place, but they didn't all get to the end, and they all had pages missing so that there was nothing that was complete and some holes I couldn't fill in. Once our elders are gone, all we can do is kick ourselves for not having paid attention and asked questions while they were still here.

He wrote many details: names, places, dates, and those that I checked were correct or very close. He had a remarkable memory. He was a practical man and wrote about things that he saw and did and that mattered in one way or another.

But in spite of all those details, he never mentioned his father's or his mother's name, simply referring to them as "my father," and "my mother," as we do when we talk about our parents. I was named for my two grandmothers so I knew their names. But it took some sleuthing to find the names of my grandfathers. Such a basic question and yet I never thought to ask.

Although his name was Rafał Feliks, every Polish person I knew, my mother included, called him Felek. Even I, following my mom's example, called him Felek, until the day I noticed that all the other kids called their fathers Dad.

When it came to place names, I did my best with the spellings I had been given, to verify or clarify them. But the geography of Poland was like shifting sand. In Eastern Europe, there are multiple languages layered over each other; transliterations; variations in spelling; the same or similar place names in different locations; and names would change with the changing borders and regimes. For the most part, I have left place names as my father wrote them, which would usually be the Polish name.

This book is based on my father's memoir and stories he told me throughout my life. This is not a history book. It is a retelling of his personal story that took place during some of the 20th century's biggest and most important events.

My father had an interesting life and an unusual one for an Eastern European Jew of that time. He boxed, competed in bicycle road races, and was very involved in athletics. He failed his last year of high school and had to repeat it. Nevertheless, he managed to attend the Medical Faculty of the University of Montpellier and then the Institut Agricole d'Algérie to study agronomy. While in Algeria he spent time with Sephardic Jews in a small desert town where he met sheiks, rode Arabian horses, and helped establish a Maccabi sports club. He was fluent in Polish, Russian, French, Spanish, English, and spoke some Kazakh, but it was Russian that he preferred for swearing. He survived the Second World War and the Holocaust because he spent those years trapped in the Soviet Union.

I am the last member of the family. My way of keeping my father's memory, my mother's, and all the rest of my family's alive was to write this book in the hope that others will find it, read it, and enjoy it. If there are questions left about parts of these stories, unfortunately it is too late to ask him to clarify.

4

Childhood

The Park

His earliest recollection was pushing his perambulator in Ogród Saski (Saxon Garden), a 38-acre public park located in central Warsaw. This was in summer 1913, and my father was not yet two years old. He didn't want to sit in it and be pushed by his parents. Any effort to get him to give up his first attempt at physical exercise was met with his crying "*samutko*," meaning "by myself."

My father was Rafał Feliks Buszejkin and his recollection was second-hand. It was something his mother had told him when she considered his stubbornness, which she said came from the milk of his "*mamka*." She was not talking about her own milk. She had developed a breast infection so they had engaged a peasant girl to be his wet nurse. For more than a year, his *mamka*, Walera, supplied him with milk and stubbornness in abundance.

I remember once when I was grown and he came to visit me in Berkeley and I said something to him about his being stubborn. He said, "Me? Stubborn?" Little did I know then that his mother had been telling him all along.

Ogród Saski was founded in the late 17th century and opened to the public in 1727. Not only is it the oldest public park in the city, it is one of the first publicly accessible parks in the world, made public even before Versailles. Dad didn't remember the perambulator, but he never forgot the park, and writing when he was 67 years old, he said that Warsaw was the greatest city in the world.

Abram

My father's father, Abram Buszejkin, was born into a family of well-to-do foresters in a small town in the Polish Ukraine. Abram's father bought forests, engaged lumberjacks, and sold the timber to sawmills. Abram's early education was at a cheder. He spoke Ukrainian, Russian, and Polish, and at home they spoke Yiddish.

When he was 13, after his bar mitzvah, Abram asked his father for permission to go stay with his uncle in Warsaw. Apparently Abram was also stubborn. He waited a year, and when he was 14, his father did finally give permission and Abram was put on a train to Warsaw, which at that time was part of the Russian Empire.

At his uncle's house, they spoke Polish at the table where they said no prayers and did not cover their heads. After his first supper with the family, his uncle took two blankets, a pillow, and led Abram to his store, which would be his place of work and his home.

The uncle owned a wholesale textile store on Nalewki Street, (now called Bohaterów Getta, Heroes of the Ghetto). The neighborhood was inhabited mainly by Jews, and Nalewki Street was an important thoroughfare that had been painted by Canaletto in 1775. Abram spent two years working for his uncle and sleeping on a table in the shop.

In those two years he studied with his cousin and mastered Polish and Russian, as well as algebra, trigonometry, and history. He also managed to save money from his small salary, so at the end of two years he disappointed his uncle when he quit his job to attend the last two years of high school, using his savings and supplementing it with income from tutoring.

During his two years of school he would go with his cousins at Christmas time to visit another branch of the family that lived in Nieśwież, in the occupied Polish region of Belarus. It was his first experience of leisure activities. They went dancing, skating, and eating out in restaurants.

One night at a private dance, he met a beautiful, slim, blond girl with two long braids falling down over her shoulders. It was love at first sight.

Abram cut a fine figure. He was well built, dressed in the uniform of his school that resembled a military uniform, and he sported a pince-nez. But he couldn't master skating and after some futile attempts, decided to join those who were admiring the skaters from the side.

In the center of the ring was a couple that attracted everyone's attention. The man was tall and very handsome. The pair wasn't just skating, they were flying over the ice to the music of the Blue Danube. While waltzing, her long blond braids were also flying, almost parallel to the ground. Everyone backed away to make room for them. Abram asked his cousin who the handsome young man was and was told he was one of Count Radziwiłł's sons. You could see their castle from any part of town. The girl was the beautiful blond he had fallen in love with the night before. Abram was jealous.

He spent the next summer in Warsaw tutoring to save money so he could go to Nieśwież again at Christmas to see his girl. The romance developed nicely and before leaving Nieśwież they were engaged with the blessings of her parents. Sonia was 14 and Abram was 17. He finished school at the end of the term and worked hard the next seven years in order to be financially ready. They were married in 1909.

After finishing high school, he accepted the position of salesman at his uncle's and worked in that position for four years. During those four years he saved money and then went to Liege, Belgium where he worked and studied as a textile technician for the next three years. After his return to Poland, he and Sonia were married and went to live in Warsaw at 26 Nowolipie Street where Dad was born three years later.

Abram tried to go into business but had no success, so he started to tutor pupils in order to build up his capital. He tutored in all subjects for a high school diploma including Latin and Greek. He had so many students he had to have them doubled up in their apartment. It was a lucrative business and in 1913 they moved to a larger apartment on Elekhalne Street.

Sonia had two brothers: the older, Michael, and the younger, Noi. By that time both of them had graduated high school and they came to live with the family to facilitate continuing their studies. Michael entered medical school and Noi studied business administration.

Moscow

It was 1915 and Dad was three years old. The First World War had broken out, and he and his parents, Abram and Sonia; Sonia's father, Solomon Myszkowski; her mother (whose name I don't know); Sonia's brother, uncle Noi; and her aunt Róża's family, the Szmuraks, all left Poland together and moved to Russia.

They went first to Pesochive, a small town near Moscow, and waited there for permission to enter the capital. In those days, Jews still needed special permission to live in Moscow, although this restriction was soon to come to an end. The city was beyond the Pale of Settlement, a demarcation instituted by Catherine the Great in 1791 that prevented Jews from living in certain parts of the Russian Empire, notably Moscow and Saint Petersburg.

Dad's memories of Moscow were of snow and that it was shoveled every morning, leaving white mountains that would reach almost to the roofs of the single-story houses. In the sun, the snow sparkled like a thousand stars. There were Russian Orthodox churches with golden domes every three blocks. He used to make the sign of the cross when he would pass one because all the other kids did. His parents would laugh at that, but never explained why it might be inappropriate and they never forbade it.

They used to visit a family with three young girls about Dad's age and there he also met a boy called Pyetya. The five of them had two favorite games: "train" and "papa and mama." In train, the tallest of the three sisters was the locomotive and the rest of them were the wagons, each holding the one in front by the shoulders and moving between the furniture all around the apartment on what would be the railroad tracks. In papa and mama, the girls would lie like sardines on the sofa and the two boys would lie on top of them crosswise. The oldest girl told them that she had seen this done by her mother and father. This was the girls' favorite game, while train was the favorite of the boys.

The family lived on the first floor of a four-story apartment building on Kudrinskaya Street, a few houses from a big square. The Szmuraks – his mother's aunt Róża, her husband Samuel, and their three children, Fenia, Rafał, and Fira – lived across the hall. Fira, the youngest, was three years older than Dad.

Between the street and the building there was a garden and that was the domain of the children.

Nearby was a big department store – a memorable department store, because that is where Dad's parents bought him an important toy. They went there together, and they returned home with a hoop and stick. It was a toy he never forgot.

Even as a child, Dad enjoyed working as much as playing. He said that preparing their double-paned windows for winter by lining them with moss and sealing the frames with homemade paste made of flour and water was fun. But was it more fun than the hoop?

Windows were not only for work; they also served as the playing field for a game. This game was also called trains. In this one, which Dad said was his favorite pastime, you would spit on the glass and watch the saliva run down. That was the train. More spitting meant more trains, and it took a lot of ingenuity to keep the traffic in order and prevent collisions.

Summer games were outdoors. There was a pail of old bricks in the garden which they would use to build two castles. Then, lying behind the castle wall, they would throw small rocks across at the adversary.

One day his cousin Rafał took him to see Maurice Maeterlinck's play *The Blue Bird*. Said to be one of the most iconic plays of the Russian theatre, it was first staged in 1908 by Konstantin Stanislavsky and was a kind of precursor to *The Wizard of Oz*. Dad didn't understand what was happening on stage, but from their perch in a high balcony, possibly in the Moscow Art Theatre, he was impressed with the multitude of people assembled in the big theatre, all silent while the action on the stage was vibrant and loud.

When the performance was over and they were coming downstairs, Dad noticed other theatres through the open doors that had a similar stage with the identical curtain and he asked Rafał why they had gone to the highest theatre when there were two theatres below and they would not have had to climb so many stairs. Rafał tried to explain that they were all the same theatre with different levels for the public to sit, but Dad was sure he was not telling the truth. After all, when he went to visit his friend Kolya who lived above them on the second floor, he couldn't see his own apartment from there.

While they were living in Moscow, in the summers they would go to Yevpatoriya, a major port, rail hub, and resort town on the Crimean Peninsula. There, Dad's father would rent a small sail boat and Dad could hold the helm. Dad loved going sailing; he loved seeing their white sail against the deep blue sky and sea. Once an ocean liner almost crushed them, but his father saved them both with his navigating skill. "Don't tell anything about it to your mother," he said. It was their first common secret and made Dad feel much closer to his father.

There were great piles of salt on the beach and chicken burgers for lunch. These were prepared by the cook at the pension where they stayed and were made especially for Dad at the request of his mother who would say to him "Fala, eat the kotlet to the end." That saying stayed with him all his life and also became famous among his friends. In high school, friends would come to eat and leave with that in their head. Years later, in 1967, he received a letter from his old friend Aleksander Pacho, then vice minister of health in Poland, who, after all those years, remembered and quoted his mother's admonition.

Revolution

One October morning in 1917 there was a tremendous noise outside, and his father did not go to work. Instead, he gathered everyone in the family and, to my father's delight, put them all into the bathroom and told them to stay there and wait. He was back in an hour. The Bolshevik Uprising had begun.

That evening all the tenants of the building came to the Szmurak's apartment to discuss what to do about possible plundering, robberies, or the murder of civilians by bands of hoodlums. A committee of defense was appointed, but no plans for defense were developed nor were any arms obtained. The only achievement was the hanging of a large copper pan, normally used to make preserves, from a chandelier in the foyer. This, together with an accompanying hammer was to serve as an alarm.

Instead of going to bed at eight as usual, that evening Dad and his cousin Fira had stayed up and listened to the grownups until late into the night. Dad didn't understand much, but Fira explained it to him the next day. And she had a plan. "Give me your word that you will keep this secret." Dad agreed. "This evening after supper we will go down to the foyer and bang the hammer against the pan and then see what happens."

Dad was amazed and terrified by Fira's audacious plan. But she insisted, probably because she didn't want to take all the responsibility, and he had given his word. And so after supper, they met in the foyer and started banging. The noise was deafening. Then they hid behind the door that led to the cellar, leaving it slightly ajar so they could see what would happen next.

They waited. Nothing happened. They hadn't worn warm clothing and were starting to shiver. Finally they decided to return to their respective apartments and take their punishment.

The next morning it all came out. No one had done anything. The adults were ashamed, everybody laughed, and Fira and Dad were heroes!

Two weeks later he overheard his father talking with the rest of the family about two horses and two wagons and traveling at night. The next day, his mother started to pack. They couldn't take everything, and Dad's hoop would not be coming with them. The next night he was awoken by his mother, dressed, and put into a wagon with the rest of the family. The Szmuraks were in the other wagon.

For the next few weeks they traveled at night through forests, avoiding any towns, villages, or the main roads. Dad was frightened, even though his father, who was the driver, gave him the reins to hold from time to time. He saw half of a dead horse lying amongst the trees. His grandfather explained that the other half had been eaten by wolves.

He was five, and he was afraid of the wolves. His grandfather told him not to worry and told him a story. One day, back in Poland, he found himself in a dense forest when three wolves stopped in front of him on the path. Not thinking for long, he pulled the sleeve of his jacket down to protect his fingers from the wolves' teeth, put his whole arm through the mouth of the wolf, deeper and deeper through his chest and stomach and when his hand passed out the wolf's ass, he grabbed its tail and with one, brisk movement, pulled the animal inside-out. The other two wolves, frightened to death at seeing their friend's bowels hanging out, fled and he never saw them again.

This is a story you will hear from many people who lived in that part of the world in the old days. It tends to come in one of two versions with the poor eviscerated creature being either a wolf or a bear. In any event, this version did not make Dad feel any better. In fact it made things worse because now he started to imagine the two wagons surrounded by dozens of wolves, all with their bowels hanging out.

Minsk

Dad didn't remember how long it took them to get to Minsk, in Belarus, traveling only at night, but it must have been about three weeks. There he found wooden sidewalks and muddy streets. They lived on a street that sloped down toward a river with a wooden bridge. Their apartment was on the first floor; the Szmuraks rented an apartment on another street.

One day his mother gave him money for a movie. His uncle Noi took him there and was supposed to pick him up after the show. All Dad remembers of the film was that there was a man walking on a narrow board high above a tank with something boiling in it, and the bad guy pulled a lever and the man fell in. At that moment, Dad had a strong urge to go to the bathroom. He remembered the two large outhouses in the center of the square in front of the movie theatre and with considerable difficulty he found his way out, reaching the outhouse in time.

When he got back, the woman at the entrance wouldn't let him in because he didn't have his ticket. He explained that he didn't know where he had put the ticket. "Why didn't you use our indoor facility?" she asked. "I didn't know they exist," he yelled back. At that point the manager came, heard the story, and let Dad in.

To Dad's surprise it was a different film with different actors. There were fields and horses and a blond girl. When the film was over and he went out, he found Noi running up and down the street looking for something. It was Dad he was looking for. Dad had come out of one movie house and went back in to the one next door. The movie at the first theatre had finished fifteen minutes before and Noi was frantic, sure that Dad had been kidnapped.

One bright morning Dad's father told him to put on his good suit, and they went walking to a school that was about half an hour away. It was a tremendous building with a lot of boys, some of them wearing the complete school uniform: a dark blue jacket with silver buttons and a thick belt with a shiny brass buckle. Dad asked his father if he could wear such a uniform. "If they admit you, you will have everything including a dark blue cap with white trim and the school emblem on it."

Dad was in seventh heaven but worried about being admitted. He was six but the minimum admission age was seven and all the other boys were taller than him. It was a preparatory school that was followed by eight years of high school. But a miracle happened, and he was admitted. They had only a few days to prepare everything: go to the tailor to have the uniform made, buy a belt, black shoes, and the cap.

On Christmas Eve, Uncle Noi took him to school and left him there so he could recite a short poem. Other boys were reciting poems, singing, playing instruments, while he was standing by the huge Christmas tree waiting for the teacher to tell him when to start. Eventually people started to leave and only half were left when all of a sudden he saw the teacher, but she did not see him. So he pulled on her skirt yelling "My poem, my poem!" She stopped those who were still there, took him by the hand back to the tree, and introduced him and his poem and luckily he hadn't forgotten it. When he finished he received a loud applause, the loudest and longest was from Noi who had come to pick him up.

The first tragedy in Dad's life happened in Minsk when his uncle Michael died. Michael was Sonia's other brother, the medical student. He came down with appendicitis and had to be operated. But the doctor forgot to remove one of the surgical instruments and after a few days, Michael died. It was Dad's first experience of death.

One evening, after supper, the whole family was assembled at the table, waiting. Dad didn't know what they were waiting for, but soon enough a Polish lieutenant and his orderly arrived. The lieutenant was wearing a beautiful grey-blue uniform, high, shiny boots, a long sabre on his side, and a pair of spurs that made the most beautiful music with each of his steps.

Lieutenant Bogusław was in the Polish Haller Army. He had the face of a young girl, always smiling and very timid. He never asked for anything and even with his orderly he was more like a friend than a superior. He would often let Dad wear his cap and his belt with the sabre.

One evening Bogusław said he was moving out with the army and advised Dad's parents to do the same as soon as possible. Soon afterwards, he went with his mother to their neighbors, their maid carrying a large portrait of Dad. It had traveled with them from Poland, but now was being taken to the neighbors for safekeeping. Right after that, the family was on a train back to Warsaw.

Świder

They didn't stay in Warsaw but continued on to Świder, a resort within the municipality of Otwock, 24 kilometers from Warsaw, where Uncle Szmurak had a villa that he had bought before the war. Villa Wirunia was situated along the railroad tracks, close to the station. There were four apartments at the villa. The uncle and his family lived in one, Dad's family took the next one, and the other two were for rent. His neighbor in Villa Baranstu, Mr. Beronski, kept bees and sold honey. On the other side was a gardener with two acres covered with flowers that he sold.

Because there were no restrictions there, Jews were able to purchase property in Otwock. The first Jews started to settle there at the end of the 19th century when it was already a thriving health resort and holiday destination for the residents of nearby Warsaw. This had been made possible by the opening in 1877 of a new railway line.

In 1880, Michał Elwiro Andriolli acquired part of a farm and decided to set up summer accommodation. In 1885 he moved four wooden, richly ornamented pavilions from the industrial and farming exhibition in Warsaw. Following his death, 14 summer cottages were erected and the colony was named Świder.

Isaac Bashevis Singer was one of many Jews who spent summers at Świder, staying there in 1935, on the eve of his departure for the United States. Years later he wrote:

"There is a small town of Otwock located a dozen or so kilometres from Warsaw. It was famous all over Poland for its crystal clear air and sanitariums for those suffering from lung illnesses. (…) Kilometres of pine woods, air filled with the smell of resin; this was the place where Jews constructed their houses also called villas. They were wooden, painted brown, had to have a veranda; almost all of them looked the same. (…) In the summer Otwock and neighbouring villages were destinations of thousand families. (…) It is hard to imagine that there are no Jews anymore. The only thing left is sand."

The first days in Świder were difficult because Dad spoke only Russian and had to learn Polish. But after a few weeks, he could speak like a native.

Without necessarily intending to, Dad turned out to be a polyglot, speaking Russian, Polish, French, Spanish, and English.

One of his new friends was Stasiek, a boy his age and the son of a railway guard. They lived about half a mile away where the cobblestone road crossed the tracks. Each morning Dad would go with Kasia, their new maid, to buy goat's milk, and then he would remain to play with Stasiek and watch his father opening and closing the level crossing gates and holding a green flag for the oncoming train. "My father can stop any train, any time, even the Constantinople Express," Stasiek told him. Dad was proud to be a friend of the son of such a powerful man.

Stach, Fira, and some of the other kids would come to their villa to play croquet. They also went to the beach, about a mile away, where the Świder River, a tributary of the Vistula, ran almost dry with only about two or three inches of water in the summer. Świder means auger or drill. It is a lovely, winding river, constantly turning, making it attractive even when it runs shallow and captivating in the morning when the mists rise. The kids would build castles with complicated fortifications and tunnels in the pure, white sand.

But their passion was to collect used train tickets. Those were made of stiff cardboard, printed in advance, and had a small hole in the center. They were of different colors and some had an extra diagonal stripe. Some of the kids had hundreds of them, beautifully arranged in small boxes. They would buy them, exchange them, and play with them, laying them on a table and if you could cover your adversary's ticket, you could take the whole lot.

It was at Świder that Dad was introduced to philately by two brothers, Felek and Mietek Borenstein. They also introduced him to a philatelic club in London. Dad joined and received a catalog with addresses from all over the world and codes with which you could select certain letters describing what stamps you might need, translated into many different languages. He corresponded with several philatelists, including a doctor in Nagasaki.

Both of his parents were good on horses and that summer his father taught Dad to ride. They would rent horses each week, preferring the hot-blooded ones. After a few weeks, Dad was riding well. Once, when he was riding a dappled Arabian, he had to stop at a railroad crossing. The train was very close and the noise was overwhelming. Dad's horse became frightened and started to buck. It took a minute or two before he quieted down by which time Dad was covered in sweat. He was riding on an English saddle and had no horn or anything else to hold on to. When his ordeal was over, one of the people who had witnessed the scene approached him. He was an army colonel who told him "Nicely done. You'd do well in the cavalry." Riding was something that would serve him well in the coming years.

The idyll of that beautiful summer came to an abrupt end when the Soviet army approached from the east. Hearing the artillery, his father decided to evacuate the family to Warsaw. He said that the Reds would never cross the Vistula River, and they never did.

Warsaw 1919

When they first arrived back in Warsaw, they rented a second-floor living room with a balcony on Nowolipie Street. They had five-rooms of furniture plus personal belongings in Warsaw, but it had all been lost by the storage company and they were not compensated. Since his parents were not able financially to establish their own apartment, they decided to live in lodgings for a while. Here, Dad would occupy himself with their landlords' children making bubbles and watching them break up when they hit a passerby below.

After a few months they rented a larger room on the fourth floor at Ceglana 9. This was also a living room with a balcony, but this one was very big and had three beds, a couch, and two extra beds for guests – all in one room. The owner was Mrs. Appfelbaum, a widow with two children, Cyla, twelve, and Noldek, nine. They tried to make bubbles but the apartment was too high and they had no positive results.

There were benefits to this new location, one of them was across the street. It was a large, unattended yard behind a brick wall and was full of scrap metal. The three children spent many hours there searching for treasures. Dad struck gold with two for his collection. One was a metal coin box in the shape of a house that had a slot at the top of the chimney for the coins. The other was the skeleton of a real .45-caliber handgun. From his weekly allowance, Dad bought a lock for the coin box and asked his parents to put in any small change they could spare. The gun was too heavy for him to handle with just one hand. He cleaned it with ashes, water, and a piece of old cloth until it shined. That gun gave him real status among the boys who played in the yard.

They winter-proofed the windows as they had done in Russia and left one, the *lufcik*, a small horizontal window meant to be used for ventilation, that could be opened for fresh air. One day a pigeon flew in though the lufcik and sat on the 9-foot tall white tiled furnace. They started to leave him food on the table after meals when they left the table, and eventually he made the rounds while they ate. He became a member of the family and exercised by flying around the room, never choosing to leave through the lufcik, even when it was open. When spring came, he flew off and never returned.

That same winter Dad came down with a cold and a high fever, and he dreamt of Minsk and Bogusław in his soldier's uniform. He woke up crying. This went on for two days until the third day when his father came home with a blue jacket with shiny buttons, a cap, and a spade hanging from a belt. It was a beautiful imitation of a Haller's Army uniform. Dad put everything on, the only problem was trying to get the spade into the bed, but by the next day, his fever was gone.

Beside the metal scrap yard there was a meat packing plant that constantly emitted an unpleasant smell. Mr. Wotkowski, a big man, would come out of the plant periodically with a big kiełbasa, cut off large chunks with his knife that always hung from his belt, and give them to the kids. "How is it?" he would ask. "Excellent," they would answer. "The best," Wotkowski would finish off the exchange. The dialogue was always the same. Sixteen years later Dad would work as a cattle buyer for that company, and Wotkowski was still there.

After a while Dad came to understand why they had made the move from the smaller to the larger apartment when visitors started to arrive. Spinster friends of his mother came looking for husbands. Renegade uncles came escaping unwanted wives. Friends and relatives came, mostly from the eastern part of Poland: Wilno, Nieśwież, Baranowice, and Lida.

The first time the doorbell rang, Dad went to open it and saw a pair of very long legs in very tall shiny boots. Looking further up he observed a very long mustache the color of straw and a beautiful military uniform. Dad couldn't move. The big man moved him gently aside, stepped into the hall and said "Good morning, you must be Fala," the name Dad was called at home. Behind him followed a tall, thin woman, then a beautiful young lady, and finally a young cavalry lieutenant. This was the Zukowski family.

Now the two spare beds were full: Mr. Zukowski and Witek slept in one; Mrs. Zukowski and Zosia slept in the other. They stayed for two weeks, and while Zosia would sit and play the piano beautifully, Dad had great fun with Witek who would come out to play with them on the street or in the scrap yard. The chunks of kiełbasa became bigger.

Soon after the Zukowski family left for Wilno where they had a big farm, two friends of Sonia's came for a visit. They were the sisters Olga and Eva from Nieśwież, both of them pharmacists and, having no brothers, they were the third generation to carry on the family pharmacy. Dad's father told him they were old maids. They were nice and friendly, and both had a slight fuzz over the upper lip. So now Dad knew that a lady with fuzz over her lip meant she was an old maid.

The sisters had come to look for husbands in the capital. They stayed for two or three weeks, going out every evening to cafes and restaurants: Europejski, Café Bristol, where Paderewski, and Picasso once enjoyed dining, Ziemansha, Lourse, but to no avail, and they left without husbands.

In the years to come Olga and Eva would come to visit about twice a year. Then, three years before the Second World War, Eva came alone.

She stayed only one day and the next she left for Sopot – a resort on the Baltic Sea. A few days later she was back with a very nice man. "This is my husband," she told them. They had met two days before, were married the next day, and were now going home. Yuri was also a pharmacist and he would help them with the business.

Dad looked at Eva, so happy with her eyes full of tears. But she still had that fuzz over her upper lip.

Sonia's brother Noi would come two or three times a year from Baranowice where he lived with his parents. Sonia's mother would come twice a year. She loved to go to watch Greco-Roman wrestling and once she came to see Zygmunt Breihard, the famous modern Hercules. After the performance she took Dad to meet the famous man where she plied him with questions, mainly about his diet. Many of the wrestlers in those days were Jewish. And surprising as it was to learn that my great grandmother was a wrestling fan, even more so was that in 1920s Warsaw, professional wrestling was a spectacle and sport with a large Hasidic Jewish following. They might have been looking back to the first wrestling match in Genesis when Jacob fought with the angel.

Finally, they moved to their own apartment at Grzybouska 48 A, on the corner of Zelazna St. It was a modest two rooms and kitchen on the second floor in a lower middle class neighborhood. His father commuted to Lodz where he worked in the Chimelnicki factory.

Eventually he opened a wholesale textile business of his own with a partner, Mr. Graiwer. Even though they had a live-in maid, his mother spent half a day in the kitchen preparing food and baking. In the afternoon she would go out to the cafes -- the Lourse or Ziemansha -- with her girlfriends. She would be home at six for dinner, usually with one or two of her friends.

They had visits from some of Sonia's former admirers. Aron Kayon, a pharmacist, who did not eat meat, fish, butter, or milk, and did not put sugar in his tea. Then there were Pelix and Landenberg. Every time they came they brought a big beautiful handmade *bombonierka*, a box artistically painted on china or hand-woven straw full of chocolates. Sonia collected the boxes through the years and then, when the war broke out, they went into the loft for safe keeping. Her old suitors all remained bachelors. Kayon went to Palestine in 1935 or 36. Pelix went to Australia in 1933. Lanenberg perished in 1943 or 44 in a Nazi camp.

Uncle Julian

Before the First World War, Sonia's uncle Julian, an attorney, worked for Count Radziwiłł. He married a Jewish girl from Nieśwież, had two sons with her, and in 1915 they immigrated to Russia. Then, one day in 1924, he showed up at Dad's home in Warsaw.

Shabbily dressed like everyone in Russia in those days, he started to tell his story. He left his wife because he could not take her anymore. His two sons were working as engineers in Moscow and he was sure that the future of his wife was assured as far as money was concerned. Besides, he hoped that she would find another, more suitable, man. He had a few real estate holdings in Nieśwież and Baranowice. After three or four days, he left to go to Baranowice, but before leaving he borrowed some money from Abram and bought himself a complete new wardrobe including a pearl pin for his tie.

Two years went by without any news. Then one fine morning he appeared again, elegantly dressed, this time with a diamond pin in his tie. He had sold his real estate holdings with the exception of one house in Baranowice and decided he would go to live in Nice on the French Riviera. He set off for France the next day.

About half a year later, they received a letter from him where he described the beauty of the French coast and, at the end of the letter, a postscript mentioning that he decided to get married. The bride-to-be was a French countess.

Six months later another letter arrived where Julian announced that with his and his wife's money, they had bought an electric incubator for 8000 chickens. It seemed incubating was a good business and a sure bet. Dad's parents had their doubts.

They were right. Another half year later, Julian appeared in Warsaw. He was penniless. The business had gone bust and they lost everything they had invested. He left Nice and his blue-blooded wife and intended to settle in Baranowice. For the next three years nobody knew where he was.

Then, in the summer of 1929, he appeared at their home again and told his latest story. The last three years he had spent living with a peasant widow in a small village close to the Russian border, but this was over as he was now 62 years old.

Two years later, a friend of dad's parents from Baranowice, in Warsaw on a business visit, gave them news about Julian. He was now living and working in Baranowice as a well-to-do butcher. It seems that Julian had fallen in love with the butcher's wife, took her from the butcher, and married her. They were living in his house, the last remaining possession of his former golden times.

Cousin Solomon

Sonia had an aunt who was married to a man named Chaim Pelix who had the biggest forest plantation in the region and was a millionaire. They had two sons: Jacob and Solomon. Both boys were sent to study in Switzerland where they finished high school. Jacob, the older one, became a professor of political science at the University of

Zurich. The younger one, Solomon, was still a student at the university.

In 1917 the Russian Revolution broke out and the senior Pelix was chopped to pieces with axes by his workers. Solomon, no longer getting money from home and refusing help from his brother, left Switzerland and went to France.

In the late 1920s Solomon appeared at Dad's home in Warsaw. He told them that he was working as a longshoreman in Marseille. He had mastered French, but it was time to find a wife so he came back to Poland to look for one. He spent a few weeks in Warsaw with Sonia and her girlfriends helping him, but it was all in vain. So he finally departed for Wilno, the capital of Polish Lithuania, where he had many relatives and friends.

News came that friends had found Solomon a wife. She was a nice looking, younger girl, and her nouveau riche parents were glad to have a Pelix in their family. He received a large dowry: a big apartment building with 48 tenants in Wilno, a big farm, and a few hundred acres with a mill and a lake close to Wilno. There was also a luxury furnished apartment, and a large amount of cash. Dad never saw the bride but people described her as a very young and very nice-looking lady.

About two months after the wedding, Solomon was back in Warsaw. Over hot tea with milk and cakes filled with dried fruit he told them his story.

"Sonia, I could not stand it anymore. You should have seen how she was eating, how she was handling the knife and fork at the table! But that was nothing. One Sunday we had a lot of guests and we went to take a swim at the lake. You should have seen how she jumped from the diving board! She fell like a dead duck. The next day I packed a few shirts and I took enough money to reach Warsaw. I don't want to see her and all the riches ever again. I am returning to Marseille, to my job, and to my prostitutes."

Schooldays

Felicja Buki School

In September 1920, when he was eight, Sonia took Dad to school for a qualification exam to enter the first grade. He had to write a short story on any subject. The day before he had read a book where there had been a description of a windy day and remembering that beautiful description, he wrote a short piece, titling it "Wind." He passed the exam and started off for school a few days later with a knapsack on his back and a lunch box in his hand.

The school was a private co-educational Jewish school called Felicja Buki, named after its director and located at Orla 11 in Warsaw, a 45-minute walk from his home. It was a modern school for its time, the only co-ed school in Warsaw. The scholarship level was very high, the language of instruction was Polish, and the distinguished faculty included Leopold Infeld, the physicist who later worked with Albert Einstein at Princeton, Stefan Drewiechi, who taught Polish and was a high official at the Ministry of Education, Dr. Ehrenreich, a famous historian, and their carpentry and bookbinding teachers who were the best in their field in Warsaw. It was Dr. Ehrenreich the historian who once stopped Dad when he was at the blackboard, stood up from his chair, and said "Buszejkin, that is a very unusual name. I am sure it is Tatar and Russian in origin."

But when Dad asked his father about it, he didn't know.

They were in school six days a week, Monday through Saturday from 8 a.m. to 2 p.m. taking five different classes with ten-minute intervals and half an hour for lunch. They stayed in one room, two children per bench, the same places all year, and the teachers came to them. They studied Polish, history, physics, chemistry, biology, analytical geometry, and technical drafting. From 4 p.m. to 7 p.m. they had elective subjects like carpentry, bookbinding, sewing, physical fitness, chess, and reading room. There was no Greek or Latin and no time for mischief.

Unlike other schools, they had no uniform and were free to wear what they liked, as long as it was neat and clean. The only unifying piece of clothing was a beret with the silver inscription, "RMP," which stood for *Razem, Młodi Przyjaciele* or "Together Young Friends," a motto taken from the poem "*Oda do Młodości*" by Adam Mickiewicz, one of the most famous and beloved Polish poets.

His first school buddy was Dzideh Strumfels who passed his qualifying exam together with Dad. Dzideh lived nearby, on Zlota 27 and they would walk to school together. Some of the friendships he made there lasted a lifetime, that is, for those who were fortunate enough to survive the Holocaust that would begin 19 years later.

In his first year, Genia, one of the girls, died. It was the first time Dad had lost a friend. The funeral was in the morning and that evening Dad's parents had tickets that they had bought in advance for the Mroczkowski Circus. Dad went but the whole performance was screened out by Genia's face. It took months before he could stop thinking of her death and her face.

Through the sixth grade, Dad was an average student. The only academic subject that interested him was physics and he liked the elective subjects in the afternoons. But he attended classes, did his homework, only he did it without enthusiasm or ambition.

There were always birthdays to celebrate among the school friends. At one birthday party, when they were in the first grade, Dad was sitting on the couch next to Helenka Neufeld when Mrs. Neustadt, the mother of his friend Srymek, came in, looked them over, and said "I wish that twenty years from now all of you kids will come together like today to celebrate birthdays." Twenty years later they were in the second year of World War II. Mrs. Neustadt died in the first days of the war, killed by a German bomb, but from the time of his return to Poland when the war ended, he always remained in contact with Helenka Neufeld.

Miedzeszyn: A Country House

Every few weeks Dad would catch a cold and go to bed with a fever. His height was normal for his age, but he was very skinny with a very pale face and pale hair. He didn't have the strength and endurance that his friends had and would get tired quickly when playing outdoor games or exercising in the gym.

He did continue riding horses. Twice a month his father would take him to an equestrian center where they could ride indoors, and his mother introduced him to ice skating. She was an excellent skater, admired by Dad and all his friends, and he managed to learn quickly.

But he was not a healthy boy and his mother decided he needed more time in the country and less at school. So his father bought 2 hectares of land with a beautiful two-bedroom wooden house in the village of Miedzeszyn. There were fruit trees, and the earth was the kind of sand so typical of that part of Poland and so good for growing potatoes. Nearby lived Michal, the caretaker with his wife Michatowa and their two boys, Stefan, a year older than Dad, and Shasiek, a year younger.

The property was about six kilometers southeast of Warsaw, between Uncle Szmurak's villa in Świder and Warsaw. They spent extended time there, and Dad went through a physical metamorphosis. Running and playing out in the sun and fresh air, and climbing the tall pines did much more for his health than the whale oil and pills that had been prescribed by the family doctor.

His mother was a good cook. They did not eat much meat but they did eat a lot of fruit and vegetables, goat's milk, berries, and she baked dark rye and other types of bread. She would roast a chicken or duck and they would have the treat of using the fat on bread instead of butter, and she made *skwarki*, (pork crackling), but she made it with the skin and fat from the chicken or duck. After that they would be given glass hot water bottles wrapped in newspaper to hold against their stomachs to alleviate the pain. She made her own dark beer and served it with sour cream. When his mother was away, his father would sometimes take him to vegetarian restaurants that would serve imitation meat. When I knew him, my dad stuck exclusively to real meat and the only vegetables he liked were potatoes.

They had a continual stream of visitors out there in the country. In addition to family and old family friends, there were some of Dad's school friends. Natek Steinberg spent almost the entire summer of 1923 and introduced Dad to photography, setting up a darkroom in the basement. He was later killed by the Germans. Michał Klepfish spent two seasons with them to help cure his ailing lungs. Klepfish became a chemical engineer and was one of the last defenders of the Warsaw Ghetto, the person in charge of making the explosives. He was killed in April 1943.

Sometimes a whole bunch would come together: Olek Kehan, Henryk Rozenthal, Izio Konblit, Menro Strumfeld, Aleksander Pacho, Michal and Nalek and Guta Berliner and Basia Levitt, two girls who were accepted by the group because they could play as hard as the boys. Aleksander Pacho became vice minister of health after the war; Henryk Rozenthal was killed by the

Germans in 1940, crossing the Russian-German-controlled border; Basia Levitt went to live in London after the war. Most of the rest vanished without a trace during the war.

Prusa High School

When problems erupted at his school between the teachers and the director, Dad was enrolled in another school called Prusa at Mazowiecka 7. Whereas Buki was a co-ed Jewish school, Prusa was an all-boys high school and the majority of those boys were Catholic. Dad and his friends from Buki were suddenly in a very different environment. Their new classmates were older, taller, and many of them worked for wages; one was a sailor in the merchant marines. So while their scholastic level was much stronger, they found that physical strength was now also important.

That was a good excuse for Dad to become even more involved in sports. He took part in track and field, winning first place in the javelin throw and placing third in the ten-kilometer run in his first games. That was the turning point in the mutual relations between the new Jewish students, and the Prusa veterans. It marked a turning point but it did not eliminate all the conflict. There were still two Prusa veterans who continued with confrontations. They were Protas and Kuzwa, and Dad was the defender of his friends who he said were rich in intellect but poor in muscles.

Once, he had a fight with Protas just before class. When the bell rang, everyone ran to their seats with Protas sitting front and center with his face still bloody. When their teacher entered the classroom, the first thing he saw was Protas. "Who did this?" he demanded. No one spoke up. "You had better tell me or I am going to report this to the principal." "I fell," Protas said. The teacher tried to get the others to tell him who had hit Protas, but there wasn't a single stool pigeon in the class.

There were times when school allegiance would take precedence and they would join forces. Once, Dad's friend Henryk was beaten up by boys from Rej High School. Everyone was outraged when he showed up in class with two black eyes and a bloody nose, and an avenging party made up of Dad, Protas, Kuzwa, and two others set out for retribution. They went to the Rej schoolyard, beat up anyone who was wearing the Rej cap, and ran off before the police showed up.

It was a 45-minute walk from home to Prusa and Dad went every day with three others. Stefan and Wanlewski were classmates. The third was the school priest whom everyone called Holy Father, even the Jewish kids. All the students liked him very much. He was about sixty years old, very tall, just under seven feet, ascetically thin, a little bent forward, and when he spoke he looked you straight in the eye with a slight smile. The three of them would take turns carrying his briefcase. He was a martyr of the Tsarist-Russian occupation; he had been tortured and his fingernails removed.

Bar Mitzvah

In 1925, when Dad was 13 he became bar mitzvah. His parents engaged a teacher who worked with him for four months, preparing for the event. After the four months, Dad could read Hebrew but could hardly understand it. The teacher also prepared a speech which Dad memorized phonetically and delivered at the Great Synagogue on Tłomackie Street. Dad and Kostia Konstanz Rozin had their birthdays on the same day and shared the event.

At the time of its opening in 1878, the Great Synagogue of Warsaw was the largest Jewish house of worship in the world. It served the acculturated members of Warsaw's Jewish community, sermons were delivered in Polish rather than Yiddish, and an all-male choir accompanied the service. It was blown up personally by SS-Gruppenführer Jürgen Stroop on 16 May 1943. This was the last act of destruction by the Germans in suppressing the Revolt of the Jewish ghetto in Warsaw.

Sports

Dad began to box in the sixth grade. His physical education teacher, Mr. Chapowski had come up with the idea of boxing as an extracurricular activity and the principal agreed, hoping it would keep the lads out of their street fights.

The school hired Yumsow Dabroski who was a former heavyweight champion and a sports reporter for *Express Poranny*, the local newspaper. At the start of the program, about 30 boys came to train. They attended two sessions a week, practicing conditioning exercises and learning the theory of boxing. After about ten weeks they started to apply their newly acquired knowledge in three 3-minute rounds. After a few evenings, only a dozen boys remained and only two of them were Jews, Olek and my dad.

He took to boxing immediately. He always knew when to block shots and when to duck and had no problem looking his adversary in the eye. His punches were fast, powerful, and landed exactly where they were supposed to. He joined the Maccabi sports club and started to box in the amateur championships.

The Jewish sports club Maccabi Warszawa was established in 1915 and suspended by the Nazis in 1939. The club had a gym and boxing hall, a playground and track, and its own marina and bathing area on the Vistula River.

Not known for their physical prowess, Jews in Poland nevertheless were sports enthusiasts. My great grandmother was a fan of Greco-Roman wrestling and went to see the fights when she came to Warsaw to visit.

As in most things Jewish, there was philosophical and political debate about which of the many clubs to join. Maccabi was Zionist-oriented. There were others that identified with the Bund, Ha-Po'el, with the right wing, with Revisionist Zionists, Folklorists, and the Communist Party. Just before the start of World War II, membership in the sports clubs in Poland numbered about 30,000. There were 190 branches of Maccabi alone.

Dad had a friend from the Maccabi who was a heavy-weight boxer with a wonderfully built body and no brains who went by the name of Finn. His real name was Fainkuchen. One day a few of them from Maccabi were walking along Poniatówka Beach (recently rated among the top ten urban beaches in the world by National Geographic).

Passing a section where there were weight-lifters, they saw a group of people who had formed a circle around a dozen heavyweight professionals, lifting a barbell of 320 pounds, two-handed over their chest. These were big guys, all over six feet tall who weighed no less than 250 pounds. Finn, at five feet ten and 190 pounds of bone and muscle, asked the professionals to let him try. He took it in his right hand and started waving it around like a toy. There was consternation from the pros and bravos from the crowd.

The Warsaw Maccabi had many good boxers at that time. There was Wysochi, Ukranski, who came to Poland straight from the Ural Mountains where he had been breaking up rocks with a twelve pound sledge hammer for the last four years,

Urkiewicz, and others. They all went to Palestine for the Maccabiah, representing Polish Jewry, and remained there.

One day Dad got beaten up on the beach. As he described it, the first blow had caught him off guard, and after that he became a punching bag. The one-sided fight only stopped when his assailant's six friends made him stop. It took three weeks for the wounds to heal, but after that, Dad had no fear.

Later that year, Dabroski came with an American scout who was looking for four or five talented boxers to take to New York. Dabroski had recommended Dad. When he came home that evening and told his parents that they might be talking to the future middleweight champion of the world, his father laughed. Not so his mother. The next day, when he was at school, she took his two pairs of boxing gloves and burned them in the oven. He quit boxing. He continued with bicycle races, running, and throwing the javelin, but his favorite sport was out of bounds for the moment.

A Storm

When Dad was 17, his contact with girls was limited to ice skating and social dancing. This was 1929 and dancing included the foxtrot, waltz, English waltz, tango, and even the Charleston and Black Bottom. Dad had his own record player and records which he bought with the money he earned from tutoring several kids, among them the Koztowski children -- two brothers and their sister who used to live above them on the fourth floor. Dad would rent a carriage, pick up his students, and they would go to one of the girls' houses, most often the home of Tusia Weingort or Marynia Elerlichster.

During one summer vacation the Koztowskis engaged Dad to spend the entire summer with the three children and their maid in a rented three-bedroom bungalow in Śródborów, not far from Świder, while they went on a trip abroad. One sunny morning, Dad decided to take the children sailing on the Vistula River. He rented a coach with coachman and two horses to take them to Karczew, where he rented a boat. He chose Karczew because it was upstream, and he told the coachman to wait for them ten miles downstream.

It was smooth sailing. Dad was busy steering and teaching the two brothers how to steer and how to remain standing. Being busy with his instructions, he didn't notice what was coming up behind them from the south. There was a big storm with dark blue clouds and by the time he noticed, it was too late. A high wind started up and all of a sudden their thirty-foot sail was torn to pieces. Dad was scared to death and started to imagine a funeral with three small coffins followed by him and the maid.

He told the children to get off the benches, sit on the floor, and hold on to the mast. Dad did his best to keep steering and stabilize the boat with his feet. He tried to reach the spot where the coachman was waiting, but the current and the wind pushed them a mile and a half further. Finally he brought the boat to shore and jumped off. The shore there was steep so Dad, holding the boat with one hand and the bushes growing on shore with the other, turned himself into a bridge and had the children climb along his back and onto the shore, telling them to go straight to the farmers' houses that they could see in the distance. At that point, Dad could concentrate on the boat. Fortunately, the peasants in the area didn't wait for an invitation and were already on their way to help with ropes in their hands.

All was saved. The children hadn't cried, on the contrary, they had been calm and quiet during the whole ordeal. An old peasant woman treated their soaked souls with hot milk and honey and a hefty portion of good dark Polish country bread. A few minutes later the coachman arrived, saying it was a miracle they hadn't drowned. He had watched the whole thing from the shore.

The peasants promised to take the boat back to the owner when the storm was over and they refused any compensation for their time, trouble, and hospitality. The four sailors went back to their bungalow in the coach, with an animal skin over their knees to keep them warm. When they got back, Dad put them all to bed and kept them there for 24 hours, giving each of them aspirin every four hours. And that was that.

Dad asked the kids to promise that they wouldn't tell their parents, and they never did. But years later, in September 1939, when the Koztowskis came down from their fourth floor apartment on Leszno Street to stay with Dad's family, to be safer from German bombs, Dad and the kids told the parents the story of the storm. He says that everyone laughed.

The Mack

The Hotel Europejski was one of the grand hotels, opened in 1857 and intended to be the most extravagant hotel in the Russian Empire. In the mid-1920s, in front of the hotel, an American came and parked a big beautiful bus like no one had ever seen before. The bus was dark blue with a yellow stripe, it had thirty-six luxurious leather seats with armrests, and it had Mack inscribed above the front grille. It sat on display in front of the hotel for several weeks and thousands of people came to see it. The American was advertising it as the Seventh Wonder of the World that could be had for $13,000. Dad's father, impressed with this fine specimen of American ingenuity, decided to buy it.

He hired a big, bulky, handsome man to be the driver. This man had previously worked for Prince Felix Yusupov, one of the men who murdered Rasputin. The same year as the bus purchase, the first paved highway in Poland was finished, replacing the old cobblestone roadway. And thus the luxurious Mack ran three times a day from Warsaw to Radom, a span of one hundred kilometers, along the smooth, new highway.

Dad had a friend, Lolek Zylberszak, who lived at Bielanska 3, almost in front of the Warsaw Opera House. He had dropped out of school and was working as an electrician. Lolek was only five feet four inches tall and weighed about 110 pounds, but he had tremendous strength in his arms and could beat anybody in arm wrestling. Dad got his father to hire Lolek to be the conductor. The first trial run was a big event. All of Dad's friends were invited for a free ride with a stop at a restaurant along the way.

Family

Sonia's aunt Róża had married Samuel Szmurak. This was the family that went with Dad's family to Russia in 1914. Samuel was probably born in Kapyl, near Minsk – the same town that Mendele Mocher Sforim, the grandfather of Yiddish literature, was from. Samuel had studied as a dentist but didn't practice. He went into business instead and made a lot of money before the First World War. When he returned from Russia, he picked up where he had left off, representing the Swiss Neff Brothers silk goods factory in Poland, and Eastern Europe. The Szmuraks had lived in luxury, and after their return from Russia in 1917, that continued.

In the early 1920s a young man from Kapyl – a distant cousin -- came to visit. He asked Samuel for financial help in order to immigrate to South America. "That is the land of opportunity. I feel I am slowly dying in Kapyl," he explained. This young man was supposedly related to Mendele Mocher Sforim.

Samuel equipped him with proper clothing, bought him passage on a boat to South America, gave him some cash, and took him to the railway station where the young man took a train to La Havre.

At the beginning of the 1930s, when the Depression started, most wholesale business was conducted on credit using promissory notes. By 1931, Samuel was facing bankruptcy, having too many promissory notes and not enough useable cash.

Dad's father, Abram, started to help Samuel by lending him money to assure future credit from the Neff Brothers' factory. But it was like throwing small rocks into a huge pit. In 1933, Neff Brothers came to Warsaw from Zurich to inspect the business. The whole Szmurak family was in a panic. Samuel asked Abram to bail him out of his financial mess, and he did. He did it by giving him all the cash he could raise, which totaled about $60,000. To do that, he had to liquidate three of his own businesses: a silk and satin factory, a wholesale ladder business, and his Warsaw-Radom bus line. It turned out not to be enough and both Abram and Samuel were wiped out. The Szmuraks lost everything: the merchandise, all their cash, the bad promissory notes, furniture, household appliances, and their two Italian Lancias. The only thing they had left was the Villa Wirunia in Świder, not taken because it was registered in Fira's name.

It was a harsh winter and the villa was a summer house, nevertheless, the Szmuraks had no other option but to go there to live. Abram was left penniless, forced to recall Dad from his agronomy studies in Algeria, and did not leave the house for six months.

The Szmurak family never regained their former financial status and style of living. Aunt Róża died after one year and was buried in the village cemetery in Otwock. Samuel started to develop a new strain of roses and raised Siberian Huskies. Rafał became a reviewer for a Russian daily paper in Warsaw. He earned a small salary but received lots of free tickets to movies which he sometimes shared with Dad.

Rafał never finished high school but took classes at the Wolna Wszechnica Polska (Free Polish University), a private school founded in 1918. Fira dropped out of the sixth grade. Nevertheless, they continued to study and maintained a high intellectual level.

Fenia married Władek Atapia an engineer who had repaired the Kierbedź Bridge after the Russians blew up the two middle spans as they were withdrawing from Warsaw in 1915. Władek also lost his factory trying to save Samuel and was in a state of mind similar to Abram.

Dad suggested that Władek start to produce spring chest expanders, used for physical fitness exercises, and Dad took charge of the sales to sport equipment shops in Warsaw.

Fira, the younger daughter, married Ceursch Thurmir, the son of a wealthy saw mill owner in Lida. She was living there at the time of the family catastrophe.

Władek went on to produce parts for Polish airplanes, but they never really got on their feet again. Then, in early April 1939, a letter came from the young man from Kapyl, now in Venezuela. By now he was very rich with a lithograph business all over the Americas and a villa in Caracas. He invited the Szmurak family to come and they all accepted except Fira and Ceursch. The young man sent money for new wardrobes and paid for their voyage. They left for Venezuela in July 1939.

Abram returned to work for two factories in Łódź and then became a representative selling textile goods in the south of Poland. Later he rented machines and started a small textile factory. In the final year before the war, he concentrated mostly on sales, but never recovered financially. But his health and disposition were good, whereas Sonia's health was poor with frequent visits to the doctor.

High School Friends

Henryk Rozenthal was Dad's best friend for most of high school. He had a good sense of humor, was a good student, very intelligent, a good mathematician, and a bit of a grifter. He came to Warsaw from a small town near Lublin where his parents had a small store. They were poor so Henryk lived with his aunt and uncle in Warsaw where, before school, he would deliver big bundles of newspapers to stands on his bicycle.

At lunch time Henryk would get some of the girls to share sandwiches with him. He didn't find it difficult to get Renia Sztabzyc to eat a little less because even though she was blond and good looking, she was a little bit on the heavy side. Lilka, and Stenia Bonder were sisters whose father had a delicatessen. Turning over some of their lunch allowed Henryk to eat culinary delights.

When Henryk graduated from high school he started living with Renia while completing a civil engineering degree. In those days, a man sleeping with a woman without marrying her was taboo. After finishing school, Henryk married someone else, the daughter of a prominent physician. Dad never forgave him. Henryk was killed by the Germans at the start of the war.

Adek Levin was a romantic type. He had crushes on many girls, but never married. Actually the girls all married someone else. He remained in Warsaw after the German occupation, living with his parents ten houses from Dad on Leszno #76. He lived in the Warsaw ghetto for a time, then, acquiring false papers, he became Yoseph Cedro. He was captured by the Germans and sent to one of the camps. By the end of the war he had spent time in five camps and was undressed for the gas chamber three times, but ended up surviving, and came back to Warsaw in 1946 where Dad met him again. In Warsaw he married Helenka and helped her to finish medical school at Warsaw University. They immigrated to Israel and had two daughters.

Heinek, who was older than Dad, dropped out of school when he was about 17. He lived on Solna Street on the second floor in a modest two-bedroom flat with his sweetheart, a prostitute by the name of Basia. Some of Dad's friends used her services. Maybe Heinek was her pimp, or maybe they were simply lovers; their romance had started in 1926.

Sometimes when playing hooky, Dad and his friends would visit both of them in their modest flat. It was cold inside, all his parents' furniture had been sold piece by piece until the only remaining piece was a double bed. That is where you could usually find the couple, in a cloud of cigarette smoke, covered up to their noses under thick blankets so as not to freeze because they had also sold the double-paned windows from all the rooms.

Dad met them on the street in the mid-1930s. They were nicely dressed, walking arm-in-arm, and smiling. Warm and friendly, they told Dad they had been married for two years. They wanted to go to Israel. Years later Dad found out that they were indeed living happily in Israel and they had two children.

Edward Tempilouski was Dad's age, and they were in the same class at Prusa when they were 17. Edward shaved his eyebrows and wore a hand-made beauty mark on his left cheek. He was a pimp with two girls walking the streets.

Late one evening in 1930, coming home from the Qui Pro Quo cabaret with his parents, they came upon Edward and his two girls. Even though it was dark on the gas-lit street, Edward recognized Dad. He took off his beret, bowed with a sweeping eighteenth century flourish, and said "Good evening friend," "Good evening to you," replied Dad. "Who was that!" his father asked as they walked away. "That is my schoolmate Edward who makes his living off of his two girls." His parents didn't know what to say so they didn't say anything and never referred to it again.

Playing Hooky

In his last year of high school, Dad managed to attend class only eight times the whole year. Those eight days were when his father gave him the money to pay school tuition. The rest of the days he played hooky with a confederacy of wayward youth.

Depending on the day, there would be 15 or 20 of them, and they met in the attic of the school. Their daily curriculum usually began with a game of low-stakes poker. Then they would move on to renting boats and racing on the river, or get up to some kind of mischief.

In those days, at the Boguslawski movie theater they would show films related to high school curricula that student groups could attend for free if accompanied by a teacher. Dad's hooky group went one day with Stefan, one of the older members in the role of teacher, sporting his Borsalino hat. The film that day was about unicellular organisms and was very interesting. They learned about asexual propagation, the division of chromosomes and their migration to the two poles of the cell. The structure of the nucleus and the protoplasm on a big screen was awesome. Dad was enjoying all this when all of a sudden Protas, who was sitting beside him, told him that Stefan wanted them to assemble at the back of the second balcony.

Stefan had a plan. They were to go in pairs, unscrew all the lightbulbs, and put them into their satchels. Each pair had a stronger guy and a smaller guy who was to climb up onto the shoulders of his partner and unscrew the bulbs. If anyone asked what they were doing, they were to say they were electricians fixing the lights. Once their work was completed, they left. The next day all the newspapers reported on their prank, saying it was students from out of town who had taken all the bulbs from the theater.

Theatre

Dad and his parents enjoyed going to the theatre, and Warsaw had many to choose from. There were several that they usually went to including the pre-war cabaret Qui Pro Quo, the most famous Polish literary and revue theatre of the interwar period, active in Warsaw from 1919 to 1931. It was located in the basement of what was then the Luxenburg Gallery at Senatorska 29. Teatr Polski, opened in 1913, was fitted with what was then state-of-the-art equipment including the first revolving stage in Poland. And Morskie Oko, another cabaret, as a contrast to Qui Pro Quo, was known for musical success and extravagant visual spectacle.

With his friends, he would go to the movies, but once he went with his parents to see Al Jolson in a talkie. His cousin Rafał Szmurak, who worked for a Russian-language periodical in Warsaw, had obtained free tickets and charged them four złoty apiece. Afterwards he asked if he could borrow Sonia's ring with a blue stone just for the evening. He never returned it.

Spring and the River-Lovers

Sunshine started to melt the snow and the world became warmer. It was spring and every year on the 15th of April, rain or shine, (or snow), Dad and some friends would go for a swim on the Praga side of the Vistula -- the east side -- where the water was deeper. There was Milek Stiklawski, a guard from the national bank, and three or four others. In addition there were four people who would take a swim every morning all year round. They were Trat and his wife, a city policeman, and a Jewish guy who was a furrier.

The guard from the bank was an interesting case. He never wore socks; instead he wrapped cloths around his feet and wore shoes without laces. He was grey and bald. Clothed he looked to be 60, but when he appeared in his swimming trunks, he had the body of a 20-year-old. When he was 42, he started to train. At 49 he was representing Poland in Greco-Roman wrestling and at the Olympic Games in 1928 he received a bronze medal. He was a friendly guy, did ten to fifteen rounds without intervals for relaxation, each time with a different partner. He was a vegetarian, didn't smoke, didn't drink, didn't do girls. His portrait, nude, sitting on a chair, was exhibited at the Zachęta, National Gallery of Art in Warsaw.

Podbrodzie

In 1930, Dad's grandmother, the sweet old lady who liked Greco-Roman wrestling, died, leaving his grandfather alone. By then, Noi was married and his grandfather went to Wilno to live with him and his wife Monic.

In the summer of 1930, when Dad was 18, they went to visit uncle Noi who was summering with his wife at the village of Podbrodzie near Wilno. This was a beautiful small village situated in a valley surrounded by rolling hills that were covered with pine and whose 800 Jews made up about a third of the population. There he quickly made friends with the three dozen other kids who were vacationing.

Dad had some lasting memories of Podbrodzie. The first had to do with a girl who was after him from day one. He didn't remember her name, but he did remember that she taught him how a boy is supposed to kiss a girl.

There were two twin sisters there: Marie and Tania Axelrod. No one could tell one from the other so they used to call them Maria-Tania, and left it at that. There was also a guy called Mulie Wulfin who, a few years later, was suspected of killing a university student in Wilno, but Dad didn't remember if Mulie was acquitted or if he went to jail.

All the kids in the group had bicycles except Dad, and he would run with them while they rode. However, when he got back to Warsaw, his mother took him to the Kamiński shop and got him one of the fastest road bikes. This was the second time he was in seventh heaven; the first had been that wooden hoop and stick thirteen years earlier in Moscow.

The new bike allowed Dad to take part in all kinds of races representing the sports club Legia Warszawa. Finally, he didn't have to borrow spare bikes from the club or from friends in order to compete.

Repeating the Last Year of High School

Because Dad had spent the last year of high school, playing hooky, practicing all kinds of sports, making mischief, and failing all his classes, he had to repeat the year. So the second time around he applied himself to studying for exams with Kuba Werthain, one of his best friends. At that time they lived at Elektoraina Street 14. Kuba also lived on Elektoraina at the corner of Biała. Kuba was a poet whose poetry and political satires were already being published in some of the best periodicals. They would study day and night, drinking copious amounts of seltzer water during that unusually hot spring. Kuba introduced Dad to black coffee (they only drank tea at home), and to cigarettes.

In the spring of 1931, his parents went to Świder for the season, leaving six weeks early because of the intense heat. But this time Dad stayed in the city by himself in order to study.

The day before exams, Dad proposed that they take the day off, go to the river, and go rowing, but Kuba declined so Dad went alone. He left at 9:00 a.m. and got back home at 11:00 p.m. He had rowed all day, with two one-hour rests.

Their first exam the next morning at 8:00 was Polish. Dad was familiar with the subject they were to write on and was careful to avoid certain words he didn't know how to spell. The next day was mathematics (mathematics included algebra, trigonometry, logarithms, geometry, and analytical geometry). He used all five hours and twenty-four pages of his well-prepared mathematical knowledge and could not come up with the solution to the problem. The other subjects (physics, botany, French) went well.

The results of the written exams were posted seven days later on a bulletin board. Dad passed the exams; his friend Kuba did not. It was inexplicable. Kuba was an intelligent fellow and at least as well prepared as my father. He went on to concentrate on his poetry and his writing and their contact became scarce. Although Dad passed, he had earned an F+ on the math exam. The F was for the bad result; the + was for the tremendous knowledge of the subject he had demonstrated in those twenty-four pages.

Exams over, he went to Świder to meet up with his old friends and make some new ones. That is when he met my mother, Marysia.

One morning, for lack of barbells, he was lifting heavy rocks under the bridge as he did every day, while she and two others were watching from a distance. "Who is that grey-haired man lifting such heavy rocks?" she asked. "That isn't an old man, he has light blond hair and he is our age. He is the only Jew in that bunch of weightlifters.

Mom was going with Monek Priues at the time, and Dad was also dating someone else.

High school finally finished, Dad wanted to study engineering at Warsaw Polytechnic, but his parents had other plans.

Felek, age 19

Montpellier

After repeating the last year of high school, his parents decided the time had come for him to tackle the next phase of his life as a student at the Medical Faculty of the University of Montpellier. There he raced bicycles, played rugby, and this time, managed to attend classes.

Founded in 1220, the university has a long and illustrious history. It is one of the world's oldest universities, with its medical school being the world's oldest still in operation. Nostradamus studied at the medical school in 1589 but was expelled for having worked as an apothecary, a manual trade that was banned. Rabelais took his medical degree and his portrait hangs in the gallery of professors. Since 1795, the Faculty of Medicine has occupied the former episcopal palace, formerly the Saint Benoit-Saint Germaine monastery. Built in 1364 and rebuilt to its present form in the 17th century, it is an impressive, but peculiar-looking building.

Dad was impressed by the 800-meter long Saint-Clément aqueduct, thinking it was Roman-built, from before the time of Christ. But actually it was inspired by the Pont du Gard and was built in the 18th century to carry drinking water to the city from 14 kilometers away. Palavas-Les-Flots was one of his favorite places to go to study and read. Palavas is a seaside resort, six kilometers south of Montpellier, on the Gulf of Lion and the

Mediterranean. Originally a fishing village, it was connected to Montpellier by railroad in 1872 and became a popular resort. The original train operated until 1968, and either that or his bicycle was how Dad got from town to the sea. In his day it had beautiful white sandy beaches and the few hotels were closed for the season.

The Place de l'Oeuf was the point of assembly for students in the evenings. Now called the Place de la Comédie, it was a huge oval surrounded by cafes and bistros. It had a permanent *foire*, or amusement park, where Dad went at least three times a week to practice at the shooting gallery. If you won enough coupons you received one piece of a Japanese ceramic dessert service. Dad went often enough and shot well enough to have the full set as a gift for his mother before the school year ended and kept it stashed under his bed, awaiting the trip home.

He rented a second-floor room from a widow where he had two windows that faced the street and a lovely arcade. On the same floor he found Szriek who had been a classmate in Warsaw, except that Szriek didn't play hooky his senior year, had graduated on time, and was now a year ahead.

Cycling

The two had a lot in common besides being Polish. They were both serious about their studies and both athletic. They saved enough money working as waiters at the student union for a down payment on two racing bikes, training together and preparing for amateur races. First prize would typically be a bicycle frame or 300 francs, second prize would be a front wheel or 150 francs, and third prize would be two racing tires. In those days tires blew out frequently and one had to sew the tear together along a seam on the inside. They did not yet have aluminum and the wheel rims were made of wood. The bikes had one speed and a 50/15 ratio. If you were lucky, the wind was pushing you from behind.

Szriek was an excellent sprinter and Dad had good stamina and they made a good team for long distance races. They also did a lot of touring and were able to see much of the South of France. They went to Marseille and admired the Vieux Port and Château d'If and to the Grotte des Demoiselles caves.

In Arles Dad went to the Roman coliseum and saw a bullfight. He described it as "a slow and prolonged slaughter of a proud animal," noting that the bull had no chance of surviving and was doomed to die a slow and painful death. He couldn't stand the spectacle and told Szriek he wanted to leave. Afterwards he often remembered the battered animal and what he called the human hyenas around him. Dad didn't mind a fight, but he wanted a fair fight, not a "dirty slaughter."

Dad and Szriek rode to Barcelona through the Pyrenees, a similar route to what many of those escaping the Nazis would take a decade later. On their way back he had a flat tire while still in Spain.

A peasant family invited them into their modest home where he fixed his tire and they discussed national freedom. Once he had the tire fixed, they were invited to supper with three generations of the family sitting around the table where they started off by saying grace. He described these people as proud Basques, and said their country was divided between France and Spain and how that reminded him of the partition of Poland. After supper they weren't allowed to leave. Their hosts said that it was too dangerous at night, what with cars, maybe rain, and possibly bandits.

I never knew until I lived in Barcelona that Dad had ever even been to Spain, much less Barcelona. If I had known earlier, I could have told him that he had been riding in Catalonia, not the Basque Country, and that Catalonia had also been divided between France and Spain and it was Catalans they had met and they too wanted independence. Many still do.

Dad and Szriek won a race from Montpellier to Marseille and back, about a 300-kilometer ride. One section of the race was the ride along the Canebiére which at that time was paved with cobblestones. The two Poles were used to that kind of paving, prevalent in Poland, so they gained a big advantage in that stretch. This allowed them to leave all the competitors way behind and come in first. As Dad said about the rough going on cobblestones, "*Nie ma tego złego, co by na dobre nie wyszło*," every cloud has a silver lining.

The Rooming House

In their rooming house, in addition to Dad and Szriek, there was a Polish girl on their floor, a fat girl with a face covered with acne. On the first floor lived Henri, a French student, a carpenter, and the landlady.

After about three weeks, Dad came home to be told by his landlady that he had a guest in his room – a friend who had insisted she open the door for him. To his surprise, when Dad entered his room he found Grusiko lying asleep on his bed with his shoes on. He let him sleep until supper time and then woke him up. The next day he took him to the university office and then Grusiko accompanied him to his classes. They got back at 3:00 p.m. and Dad left him in his room. It was the day before a big race with a 250-franc first prize and they needed to train.

When they got back, Grusiko had disappeared. He wasn't in Dad's room or in Szriek's. Suppertime was approaching and Dad was afraid he had gone out and gotten lost. He thought to ask the girl across the hall if she had seen Grusiko, but when he knocked on her door no one answered. So he pressed the door handle and the door opened revealing two naked bodies on the bed, one on top of the other. The bottom belonged to the girl, the top was Grusiko.

Both Dad and Grusiko were a little flustered, but the girl was calm and said, "Wait, please, in fifteen minutes your friend will be completely at your disposal." That same evening Grusiko moved in with the girl and they stayed together until the end of the school year.

One day they had a very big surprise when Josephine Baker, the famous expatriate American singer and dancer, came to their house and met with all five of them. It seems she was interested in how students of different nationalities and different races got along and was visiting students throughout the neighborhood. Montpellier had students from all over the world in every color and of every creed. There was a Hindu princess who would come to school in a Rolls Royce who sat next to a poor student from Iran who was subsidized by his government. The exceptions were members of the far right group that followed the French fascist François de La Rocque.

Unlike high school, Dad did attend his university classes. During that year he took physics, chemistry, and science. His French was good, and he was well prepared for the subjects from high school.

But one thing that gave him a serious problem was dissection. When the time came to dissect a frog, Dad couldn't take it. He never understood how it could be that he had no problem with blood when he was boxing, but cutting apart a dead frog made him nervous and ill. The poor dead frog would have a huge impact on Dad's life.

One day in the chemistry lab there was an incident when one of the students showed up drunk. They were working on an analysis, and the research formula started with the symbol L.P. (liquid primitive). The inebriated student started to shout, "I don't want liqueur primitive. I want Cointreau," and proceeded to break everything on his table.

Some of the students managed to collect him and take him to his quarters. No police, no disciplinary action. He came back to class the next day and the first thing he did was to apologize to the professor who extended his hand. They kissed on both cheeks. This was France.

Świder

At the end of the year, Dad went back to Warsaw and headed directly for Świder, the resort where his family spent their holidays and where his parents were waiting for him. He had been using French exclusively for the last nine months and for the first few days, some Polish words eluded him. But he was very happy to be home. Dad had a great love for Poland and what he referred to as "the blessings of the Polish countryside."

In a nearby villa there were two brothers. One was small, thin, and an intellectual type, the other was a good-looking, well-spoken, husky example of health, and a lady's man. Early that summer the lady's man met a beautiful girl, and they were married two weeks later. The next summer when Dad met them, the husky one was just skin and bones. Dad asked his brother about the rapid and unhealthy decline. Excessive sex, he said. Before the season was over, he was dead.

That summer, Dad met the famous Dr. Janusz Korczak. Dad had been bitten by a bee, the bite swelled, and he couldn't remove the stinger, so he went to look for a nearby doctor. Korczak managed an orphanage for Jewish children in Warsaw. At the time, he was staying in the country with them, between Świder and Otwock. When the Nazis invaded Poland, Korczak continued to run his orphanage. He was a famous figure, and many people tried to rescue him, but he refused to leave his children. When, in August 1942, the children, aged seven to fourteen, and the staff were ordered to leave and go to a collection point where they would be taken in cattle cars to Treblinka, he once again refused to leave them, saying "You do not leave a sick child in the night, and you do not leave children at a time like this." He died the next day in Treblinka with his 200 children.

Sometime during that summer of 1932, Dad broke the news to his parents that he was not going to study medicine but instead, had applied and been accepted to the agronomy program at the Institut Agricole d'Algérie.

In the Polish countryside c. 1932

Algeria

Algiers

It was fall 1932. After being sick at sea, Dad arrived in Algiers where he found a whole new, exotic world. Driving through town in a taxi he saw white buildings, palms, and tropical flowers. Men with dark faces were buying and selling things in the street, women covered their faces with scarves.

At the Institut Agricole d'Algérie he asked about finding lodgings. Most of the students were Algerian or French and most of them lodged at the school, but he found a room for less than half the going rate. The elderly owners admitted it was cheap because it was small and poorly furnished. It had a small iron bed, a small table with one drawer, and a small, unstable chair. The other part of the annex that connected to his room was where the landlady kept her chickens and rabbits. The roosters were noisy in the mornings, but he had to get up when they crowed anyway. Unfortunately, roosters do not take the day off on Sundays. It didn't look like he would be able to work, so saving money on rent would allow him to save enough to buy presents when he returned home.

You could divide Algeria into three strips. First, along the coast the land was flat with a climate similar to that of the French Riviera. Then there were the Atlas Mountains which were very picturesque and sometimes you could ski there.

And finally there was the Sahara Desert with its white sand constantly shifting. After hundreds of thousands of years, the flower-like sculptures, Rose de Sable, a selenite crystal, are formed from those shifting sands.

The school was a few kilometers from Algiers, and transportation was by bus. These were privately owned, old buses, each with a different owner. The buses looked like honeycombs and the passengers like bees. Not only were they crowded into the bus, they also rode on the roof, the fenders, and the bumpers, and trying to get onto one was a challenge. Dad rode one every day, going out to explore the beautiful city, glaring in the sun and filled with Moorish architecture and flowers and palms lining both sides of the Rue d'Isly.

But most intriguing was the Casbah. Dad spent his first day exploring the European part of the city, then he went to the Casbah at night. He summed it up as a place of semi-retirement for whores and pimps from all over the world. Many of the ladies were quite old and yet they had plenty of customers with men lining up on the street waiting. These were mostly Algerian soldiers of the French army in their colorful uniforms, looking quite handsome. They had a reputation for being the fiercest soldiers in the French army. In hand-to-hand combat they just threw away their carbines and used only the bayonets.

Dad wandered through the Casbah until midnight and then took a bus home. When he reached his chicken coop he found his landlords waiting for him by the gate. They had been worried and showed him that day's newspaper with the story of an English family, father, mother, and daughter, who had been robbed the evening before in the Casbah. Everything had been stolen from them – cameras, jewelry, money, and clothing – and they escaped only with their lives. Late that night the police found them, unhurt but completely naked, and took them to the commissariat de police.

The next day Dad met his Arab neighbors and was invited to supper. They served couscous with lamb and dried dates, and two young girls performed a belly dance. They were dressed in traditional clothes and wore bracelets covered with bells on their ankles. Couscous became Dad's favorite meal, but he never said what he thought of belly dancing.

After that he went to explore the institute's 1600 acres and was impressed. They had both modern and traditional equipment, native cattle running free and Holsteins in enclosures. Their intent was not to revolutionize Algerian farming, but to introduce new agricultural methods bit by bit by training future farmers and instructors in both methods so they could profit from the best of both worlds.

They did not study from books or printed material. They attended lectures and did laboratory work and noted everything in the workbooks that each student wrote and illustrated. The final grade was based on a written exam, an oral exam, grades from their lab work, and their workbook.

There were about 60 students at the institute, and about 75 percent of them were French, over 20 percent were native Algerians, and the remaining six were foreigners. These were János Kudelka from Hungary, Rabinowitz from Danzig, Cohen from Spain, de Grune from Belgium, Kampan from Laos, and Dad. The first three were Zionists, a noble idea, Dad thought, but completely strange to him. Most of the time they spoke Hebrew, which he did not understand, and they would march in the street singing songs. Dad and the remaining two foreigners formed their own trio, and saw each other often.

One evening Dad noticed the shadow of a middle-aged man in full military uniform covered with medals standing in Kampan's bedroom. When he asked him later who that was, Kampan said "Our king." On another occasion when de Grune asked him the same thing, Kampan answered "My father." He was a modest man and a prince.

Kampan had a car but he bought a bicycle so he could ride with Dad. One afternoon they took their javelins and rode to the beach. Standing about forty meters from each other, they started to throw when all of a sudden Dad saw his throw coming directly at Kampan and he was standing there completely immobilized, as if he were hypnotized. Dad yelled for him to move but he didn't, and the javelin pierced his right calf. Dad ran over and tied a handkerchief above his knee. They mounted their bikes and Dad pushed him until they reached a doctor.

Once, Kampan invited Dad and de Grune to a reception at the Laotian legation. Dad had no formal dress so he wore the only suit he had brought to wear on the holidays. Nevertheless, he was well received and enjoyed the treat of some very fancy food and drink.

Another time, de Grune took them to the races. Both Kampan and de Grune knew the horses and how to bet, but Dad had never been to or followed racing. So he took the program, chose a name he liked, and bet five francs. Even though he won 400 francs, he never bet again.

Dad always had sports in his life and in Algiers it was bicycling, javelin, boxing, and rugby. Once when he was looking at the posted notices of exam results, one of the French students mumbled some remark about foreign students taking over the school. He was the quarterback of their rugby team. Dad went over and knocked him down with a right uppercut. This started a melee which only quieted down when a professor arrived on the scene. Dad ended up with two broken fingers, but there were no hard feelings and he and the quarterback continued playing rugby. They went on to take second place in the North African Championship, behind the University of Tunisia.

The school also placed first in boxing at the same championship games.

Dad often went on long distance bike rides. One place he liked was La Grotte du Macchabée, in the Djurdjura Mountains on the Mediterranean coast. In addition to the stalagmites and stalactites, there was the mystery of a naturally preserved corpse that had been there for centuries and who still remains unknown. Some say he was a bandit, a kind of Robin Hood of Djurdjura who stole from the rich and gave to the poor.

My father refers to this cave as the cave of the monkeys, and although that is not its name, there are many legends and stories of monkeys in caves in that region. I especially like this one that I found at the blog *Amis du Djurdjura* because it specifically tells of another Pole.

In his book *Winter in Algiers* from 1861, Charles Desprez tells of the misadventures of a Pole who had fled his homeland which had fallen to the Prussians, had joined the Foreign Legion, then had deserted and settled on the mountain where he lived, took the name Mohammed, and dressed like the inhabitants of the country.

One night, surprised by a storm, he took refuge in a cave, but found, the next morning, that he was snowed in and trapped there with a troop of monkeys. It was very cold so Mohammed gathered branches and lit a fire. At first this frightened the monkeys, but they were cold too, so after a while they came and joined him around the fire.

Hunger began to torment him. The monkeys were also hungry and suddenly one of them disappeared and then returned with figs, nuts, and sweet acorns. Each monkey would reach out to receive his share, and Mohammed did the same. In between fire-building and eating, he would play with the young ones. Then, one morning, the snow having melted, the monkeys left the cave and Mohammed did too. He later said "I lived there fifteen days and they were among the best of my life."

Dad rode to Tipasa, once a Roman colony. None of the houses remained, but there were ruins of three churches, two cemeteries full of stone coffins covered with mosaics, the baths, theatre, amphitheater, nymphaeum, the line where the ramparts once were was visible in some places, and there were remains of the ancient harbor.

He took the advice of the natives, and when he traveled he carried a handgun – a Browning .38-caliber which de Grune gave him. Midterm, de Grune's father took gravely ill and he had to return home. He never returned, and Dad mailed him his gun in a cigar box.

Paralysis

Towards the end of the school year, Dad took ill. There had been two weeks of torrential rains in April, his room was flooded, and he needed to place bricks on the floor to be able to walk from the door to the table and to the bed without wading in water.

One rainy morning he couldn't move his legs. Finally, in the afternoon he shouted for his landlady who was out behind the well and asked her to let Kampan know. Kampan called a doctor who diagnosed an inflammation of the joints. His humid room was not a good place to stay, so he sent a telegram to his parents explaining the situation. They told him their doctor said the best thing was for him to go immediately to Biskra. This was an oasis town known for its curative facilities, four hundred kilometers away, in the Sahara. In the late 19th and early 20th centuries, it was a posh spa town, hosting celebrities such as Béla Bartok, Oscar Wilde, Henri Matisse, F. Scott and Zelda Fitzgerald, André Gide, and Karl Marx.

The next day, Kampan and a few others hijacked the bus to come and stop in front of Dad's lodgings because he couldn't move. They loaded him on and gave him a book to read on the way. It was an epic from Polish history and how they had found a copy in North Africa was a mystery. But it sat on Dad's legs while he waved goodbye to his friends.

The road was old and so was the bus, it was overcrowded, and the ride was bumpy. Making it even more uncomfortable, Dad couldn't get off at the stops even to relieve himself behind a bush, so he endured his discomfort by dozing off. Half asleep, he suddenly recognized the aroma of what he thought was gefilte fish, one of the most notable dishes of Jewish cuisine.

Looking around, he finally discovered the Arab who was eating it and asked him where he had bought it. The man told him his wife made it and offered Dad some. Dad was hungry and thirsty and didn't hesitate for a moment to accept. The generous man also gave him some tea.

They started to talk and the man asked some of the usual questions: Where are you going? What do you do? Dad explained he was a student at the institute, that he was paralyzed with a joint inflammation, and that he was going to Biskra where they were supposed to cure him.

It turned out that the Arab was a Jew, a Sephardic Jew. He worked as a tourist guide at one of the biggest oases in the Sahara, half way between Algiers and Biskra. He asked Dad about his finances and he explained that he received 600 francs a month from his parents. The man laughed and said that Biskra would cost over 600 for two days and that wouldn't include a doctor.

Bou Saâda

Bou Saâda, or city of happiness, had a Jewish population of about 2500, and the same climate as Biskra. His new friend invited him to come there and be cured, and he accepted the invitation.

With the help of a few friends, the man managed to get his live cargo from the bus into an old English Ford and taken to an adobe house where he was put into an enormous bed in a tremendous room with almost no windows. This was the home of the man's aunt, Mrs. Sonigo. The man told Dad that he would meet his younger brother, who worked as a waiter in a hotel, later in the evening. Then he and his friends bid him goodnight and good luck and disappeared.

The next morning three men came to get Dad. They took him out to the desert where an Arab was waiting, sitting under an umbrella with a pot boiling on an iron tripod beside him. The Arab buried Dad in a shallow grave, covering his body completely with sand, but leaving his head shaded by the umbrella. He gave him sweet tea to drink, and left him buried for 45 minutes. The sand was terribly hot, and he was sweating profusely. It was not pleasant. Then the three men brought him back to his bed. These were to become his new friends: Georges Djaoui, Shishiportish, and Meshishe.

This routine continued for the next four days. After the second day the pain almost disappeared, after the third day he could walk, and after the fifth his skin was peeling off in ribbons, but he was completely cured. No doctors, no medicine. He gave the Arab 50 francs, but the three friends would accept no money.

During his stay with Mrs. Sonigo, she cooked for him twice a day. Her menu did not vary and included cutlets made from calf's brains in tomato sauce, couscous, pita, and teas. He stayed with her for six weeks.

His friend Georges was about 30 years old, six foot four, overweight, strong, but out of shape. He was the regional director of an Algerian bank. Shishiportish was his next door neighbor, a young man his age and the son of the prefect of police. Meshishe was a cobbler, about 40 years old.

Through them Dad met Simon and a handsome Arab named Djabour. Djabour had a wholesale oriental rug and native art shop. Simon was the owner-manager of a business that was a café in the front, and a bordello at the back. This was the bunch he began to spend time with. He stayed in contact with his parents whose doctor in Warsaw wanted him to spend at least six weeks there in the desert.

Once he was well he started to meet people on the streets and in the cafes. In addition to the 2500 Jews, Bou Saâda had a population of 5000 Arabs plus about 150 tourists in season. Surrounded by date groves, industry included the production of jewelry, metalwork, carpets, and bousaadi knives. The bousaadi knife has a straight, single-edge blade about six inches long and was derived from or is related to the Corsican and Genovese style of knives, often called "vendetta knives." Bou Saâda was a major producer of this type of knife, hence the name. There was a textile mill and, even in modern times, it was a trading post for nomads. There was a movie house that showed films on

Thursdays, otherwise evenings were spent at a café, sitting on the beautiful carpets, sipping tea and eating exquisite pastries.

Maccabi

One evening while sipping tea at Simon's, Dad asked the group if they wouldn't like to have a sports club, pointing out that they were getting fat and doing nothing about it. They all liked the idea and it spread through the town, resulting in a town meeting where more than half the male population attended, money was raised and the idea approved. In three days they had raised over 300,000 francs and set out to buy equipment and have uniforms made. The uniforms were white shorts and blue sleeveless shirts with a Mogen David on the front. A local lawyer drew up the bylaws and they named the club Maccabi.

They organized different sports including Swedish gymnastics, track and field, bicycle touring and racing, weight lifting, and boxing. Gymnastics was open to men and women, the others were men only. Dad was busy day and night, being the only instructor. But it went well, village body fat starting to disappear, being replaced with muscle.

However, there was a problem at home, and Dad couldn't sleep. The problem stemmed from the room next to his which was occupied by a young woman, a substitute teacher, who had come from the capital to fill a vacancy of a teacher who was ill. There was a young man who was coming every night and making exuberant love with her. Dad was overworked and sleep-deprived, but he bore his cross with dignity and didn't say a word.

Eventually the couple began to quarrel and this made even more noise. Late one night when Dad was cycling home, he saw the substitute teacher walking, heading out of town into the desert, and he found the young man running around frantically looking for her. But their fights continued, going from bad to worse, and a few days later she returned to Algiers, not even waiting for the return of the other teacher. The failed love affair meant that once again, Dad could sleep at night.

One afternoon after lunch, a crowd showed up with a big, tall German man in the center. He was Rudolph Winkler from Leipzig. He had just arrived by bus from Algiers, he had his bike loaded with rucksacks front and back, and he was on a world tour, planning to leave the next morning for Biskra. The crowd had found this other foreigner and thought to have the two meet. Winkler had a camera and took some photos while he was there. A year and a half later, when Dad was in Warsaw, he received copies of those photos in the mail. They are the only photos that my father had of his time in Algeria and some of the few we had from before the war.

According to Dad, the biggest tourist attraction in the oasis was a tomb created for a Dutch painter and Winkler photographed it. But I think he mistook Dutch for French. The famous tomb is for the French painter Alfonse-Etienne Dinet. Dinet had bought a house in Bou Saâda and spent much time there painting. He also became an Arabic scholar and translated many works of Arabic literature into French. He became so enamored of the culture that he converted to Islam, adopted the name Nasreddine Dinet and made a pilgrimage to Mecca before he died, just four years earlier, in 1929.

Winkler was still there the following evening when Herman, Georges, Meshishe, and Simon proposed they go visit a very rich sheik in the mountains. They went in Simon's old Ford. Equipped with a generous amount of beer and anisette and stopping on the way to pick up Rudolph at his hotel, they headed 40 kilometers up into the mountains.

It was an unpaved, bumpy, narrow road, wide enough for only one car. They began their celebration as soon as Simon stepped on the accelerator, so by the time they arrived, they were half drunk. The sheik was tall and very handsome and gave them a guest book to sign. Perusing the pages Dad found Marlene Dietrich's signature, so he signed his name close to hers. He was a big fan.

They feasted on sheep meat, couscous, pita, and red wine. Belly dancers appeared. They ate and drank for two hours and at around 10:00 p.m. decided it was time to go back. Dad was the least drunk and he was afraid for any of the others to drive, but he had never driven a car before. However he had driven motorcycles, so he announced with authority that he would do the driving. Everyone agreed and off they went. He knew where first gear was, but not the other gears, so he drove all 40 kilometers in first gear. Nobody noticed a thing.

Dad met Ahud who was a son of another sheik. His father raised pure-bred Arabians and he asked Dad if he knew how to ride. Dad starting riding horses when he was a kid, so Ahud invited him to his father's stables. He had never seen so many beautiful horses in one place in his life. They were dapple grey with long manes and tails. Ahud chose one for him and put on an unfamiliar type of saddle. The horse took off like a bat out of hell and Dad couldn't control him. After more than half an hour, he finally stopped on top of a dune, all covered with foam. It turned out the horse had an illness that affects the ankles, provoked by the effect of the moving sand. It was a condition that came and went and happily, it never came again in the subsequent times that Dad came to ride.

The day came for the inter-club sports competition and Dad was the organizer. In the audience watching the boxing was El Houssine Jdidi, the middleweight champion of North Africa. Also there was the American boxer Maxie Rosenbloom. Partly in French and partly in Yiddish, Dad explained to him about the sports club they had recently set up. Rosenbloom was very enthusiastic and delayed his visit to Biskra where he was going for a cure for his joints. He came to watch the guys sparing and then went running with them down the streets in his fancy clothes. He promised to stay a few days for an exhibition fight with Dad so they advertised in the newspapers and put up signs in all the neighboring towns and villages. Tickets were 10 francs and they raised a fortune. Dad lost but said that Rosenbloom gave him enough leeway to "save the honor of Bou Saâda."

Georges

Georges was Dad's best friend in Bou Saâda. While Dad was living there, he introduced Georges to Mom's sister Estusia. By all accounts, Estusia was exceptional. She was intelligent, beautiful, and talented in any number of things including the piano, art, and poetry. She was living in Warsaw and Georges wrote to her there. They corresponded for years. Georges fell in love with my mother's beautiful sister, and I believe Estusia felt the same, but they never met.

When World War II broke out, Georges wanted to get Estusia out of Poland. But she didn't want to leave and chose to stay with her parents, brother Yakub, and Mom's other sister Irena. They all died in the Holocaust.

Dad managed to find Georges after the War. In the 1960s, he and his entire family went to live in Paris. I met them when I was in Paris in 1982.

There were ten people around the lunch table, his parents, their grandchildren, his brother and his brother's wife, and we ate rabbit couscous – my first couscous. The few photos my mother had of her family were the ones that Estusia had sent to Georges during their correspondence. Georges never married.

A Thunderbolt

One day a registered letter arrived from Warsaw. Dad's father was having a financial crisis and he had to return home. The news struck him like a thunderbolt. Here he was living the best part of his life – the most pleasant and fulfilling, in fact, like Mohammed the Pole seventy years before, he also counted those days in Algeria as among the best of his life. And what would happen with his studies? This was the first time he ever perceived any weakness in his father and realized that he too was human.

He left the next day for Algiers, telling only Georges that he was going. He simply could not get himself to say goodbye to everyone. He left his bicycle as a gift for the sports club, sat on the bus with tears in his eyes, and didn't look back. He was right in thinking that he would never see Bou Saâda again.

With the 900 francs he had saved for presents, he went shopping in Algiers. He bought nine bousaadi knives, the two fanciest for his father, the others for friends. He also bought five Arabic-style necklaces, but could not find anything right for his mother.

In Marseille it was the same. He couldn't find the right gift and figured he would buy her flowers when he arrived in Warsaw. He had walked up and down the Canebière when all of a sudden he spotted something beautiful in a jewelry store window. In a large box lined with dark blue velvet there was a pendant in the form of the letter "Y" hung on a black cord, composed of nine rough cut blue-green sea stones fitted with artificial diamonds in between each of the stones. There was no price, and he didn't have the courage to go in and ask. He had a little over five hundred francs left and he didn't think that would be enough.

He finally found some courage, went in, and asked to be shown the pendant. The salesman gave him an ugly look and went to get it. "How much?" asked Dad. "Three hundred fifty francs, said the man. "Could I have it gift wrapped?" asked my father. "Certainly," said the man who suddenly had turned into an angel. Forgetting about Bou Saâda, friends, school, and the disaster awaiting him in Warsaw, Dad was happy to be heading home with the proper present for his mother.

He left by train from Marseille-Saint-Charles and went to Ventimiglia where he had to change trains for the train to Milan. It was 11:00 p.m. and he had an hour and a half to wait, so he took his two valises, found a bench outdoors, and stretched out, looking at Orion up in the sky. When he woke up six and a half hours later, it was sunny and he had missed his train.

He had left Marseille with 150 francs in his pocket, and didn't eat supper before leaving in order to save money. By the time he arrived in Milan, with a four-hour wait for the international train that would take him through Italy, Austria, Czechoslovakia, and half of Poland, he gave in and spent what was left on supper at the station. He was penniless.

He managed to find a seat in the packed train. Everyone was friendly and talking, but Dad didn't know Italian so he couldn't participate. Across from him was a young man who started to speak to him in French and asked where he was going. He explained he was going to Warsaw. The young man was a Fiat engineer and was being sent by the company to Moscow to help them build cars.

It had started to feel like one big family in the wagon when at one station, a woman with a big hat boarded and stood at the entrance to the carriage. Dad stood up so that she could have his seat. This started a whirlwind of activity and all the other men stood too, insisting that since Dad had such a long journey ahead of him, and they weren't going far, that he should keep his seat. This was Italy.

The Italians were a lively bunch, talking and sharing their food. But Dad didn't want to accept anything because he had nothing to share in return. He just barely endured his hunger when, in

Kracόw, a group of orthodox Jews entered the carriage and started in eating garlic sausage. Dad had to leave the carriage until they finished their lunch.

When he finally reached home, he found that everything had changed.

Felek on the left

The Maccabi sports club in Bou Saâda, Felek in
long pants

Estusia

92

Warsaw in the 1930s

The end of his studies in Algeria when he was 21 marked the end of Dad's youthful adventures. But there would be other kinds of adventures to come. He made his way from the oasis of Algeria to Warsaw, and by the time he reached home he didn't have a penny in his pocket and found that his parents were completely broke. His father had loaned money to Uncle Samuel and had liquidated some of his own businesses to do it. But it wasn't enough and Uncle Samuel went bust, taking Abram down with him.

His father was a changed man. He greeted Dad warmly as usual, hugged him, asked about Bou Saâda and school, but then just went back to reading the newspaper. He was probably suffering from depression, but they didn't know anything about that at the time. He hadn't left the apartment for six weeks, and his mother, for the first time in her life, had taken control of things.

The Millionaire

Sonia borrowed a few hundred złoty from friends, rented out Dad's room to a young couple, and Abram's study to a millionaire bachelor who also took lunch with them. They had struggled to send him the 120 złoty for his return trip. She was hoping that Abram's withdrawal would end soon, if not, she didn't know what she would do.

At lunch Dad met Leon Fuks, the millionaire. He was a pleasant man in his forties who had made his millions buying and selling foreclosures. He told Dad that he had been waiting for his arrival because he needed an assistant and wanted to hire him. Dad wasn't sure he really needed an assistant, but he was glad to get hired, and without asking any details, he started to work the next morning. The same day he advertised as a French tutor in the newspaper.

Leon paid him handsomely, but Dad didn't think he merited the generous salary; he was sure it was a humanitarian gesture. Leon was shrewd – merciless – in business, but with Dad he was all heart.

Soon the first pupils began to arrive for French conversation. The first to arrive was a beautiful young girl of 22. A girl over 20 was an adult, and Dad wondered why she had come with her mother. More pupils came, sometimes alone, but mostly with their mothers. They were all female.

There came a point when he had more girls than time so he decided to quit working for Leon and concentrate on the tutoring; it was more lucrative and more pleasant. More students came. Finally Dad realized what was going on. No one wanted to come in the morning or the afternoon; they all wanted evening lessons. It wasn't his excellence as a French tutor that was driving them to his door, it was the possibility of meeting the millionaire lodger. He started to think about other ways he could earn money.

A Variety of Work

In those days some men still wore detachable collars and Dad had an idea for a soft collar that was comfortable and that could be attached to any shirt without having to use the studs which were special to each manufacturer. His collar was made of rubber. He set up a business, produced, packaged, and sold the collars with unexpected success.

He also set out to recover some of the money that was owed to his father. Abram had often sold to his customers on a handshake, with no payment or promissory note, and now some refused to pay. One of them owned a big retail store on Nalewki Street. Dad talked with his friend Lolek, the same one who had worked for Abram as a conductor on his bus, and together they went to talk to the man. Dad told him he had fifteen minutes to pay his debt or return the merchandise or someone would need to order a coffin for him. The man went directly to the cashier and paid up. Dad never said how much debt-collecting he engaged in, but his father did recover his health in about six months and started to work once again.

Dad did all kinds of jobs for the first three years after he returned from Algeria, including the rubber collars, tutor, youth counselor, and boxing instructor. He said that he tried so many jobs because he was searching for adventure. Finally he decided to find work in what he had been training for, but agricultural jobs were not easy to come by in the capital and he didn't want to work in a laboratory. His father was friends with the mayor of Warsaw and suggested he work for the city Department of Parks, where eventually he could have a good position even without a diploma. But he would have had to convert to Catholicism to do so and he wasn't prepared to do that.

Poldrob Ceglana

His mother and father finally got fed up with him doing all kinds of miscellaneous work and suggested he go see his father's cousin, Olek Olomucki, who was a bigshot at the Chamber of Commerce. Dad preferred finding something on his own, but eventually he called Olek who told him to come right over, they would be at home all evening. Dad went to change his clothes and pay them a visit when his father stopped him, saying he would have to bring them something. They were well-off people and had everything, so Abram said that they would really appreciate the daggers Dad had brought him from Algeria. He didn't want to give them up, but he thought it was important, and Dad thought he was right. But it sent a shiver down his spine.

Olek admonished him for not coming to see him three years earlier, and gave him a letter of introduction to Joseph Gothelf, the president of Poldrob Ceglana. This was quite a surprise as it was the meat packing plant across the street from where Dad lived on Ceglana 9 when he was eight years old and they had recently come back from Russia. This was where he and his friends used to play in front of the plant, where there was always an unpleasant odor, and Wotkowski the watchman used to give them chunks of kielbasa he would cut off with a knife.

The day after seeing cousin Olek, and reminiscing afterwards about his days on Ceglana Street sixteen years earlier, Dad went, letter in hand, to Poldrob Ceglana. Entering the factory he saw Wotkowski, as handsome as ever, now with a few streaks of grey in his hair, but the watchman didn't recognize him.

He was ushered in immediately to the boss who was in his office together with his brother Kuba, and his cousin Nolam. There were no technical jobs at the moment, but they put Dad to work in an office. He started the next day.

Eloped

Dad started going steady with my mother the summer before he set off for Algeria. During this three-year period after his return, they continued their relationship, although he called it going steady with a few intervals. In any case, he never says he fell in love with her; he says "on the final score, I wound up with Marysia."

Mom was one four children. Her father was Ignacy Sznajderman, a well-to-do furrier, and her mother was Dora Chwalibog. Her sister Irena was the eldest, then Estusia, her brother Kuba, and Mom who was the youngest. She was a very popular gymnast and dancer at the Warsaw Maccabi. The family was pleasant and harmonious, but, Dad noted, it was Estusia who towered over the others with her artistic ability in poetry and painting. She was intelligent and beautiful and very modest, "which made her an exception to the rule of the younger generation of the family." Estusia was the sister he had introduced Georges to when he was staying in Bou Saâda.

In the early thirties, Ignacy took ill with a stomach ulcer that had put him out of commission within two years, and he never fully recovered. When Dad started visiting their home, he still employed one man, a furrier, mentioned earlier, who used to swim in the river all year round, breaking through the ice in the winter.

Although she was two years younger, Mom received her baccalaureate one year after Dad. She had never played hooky. She worked at home with her sisters helping her parents by knitting sweaters. She also worked for a while as a handworker in a big store, Karibi, on Marszałkowska Street. Finally, she took dressmaking courses at ORT, the trade school, where she was the best in her class.

ORT was founded in Saint Petersburg in 1880, created to help Jews who were living in poverty. This was mainly the result of the creation of the Pale of Settlement, an area where Jews were restricted to living by Catherine the Great in 1794. Those who were living outside the Pale were removed from their homes and villages and resettled to within its boundary. This resulted in four million Jews living in a restricted area, barred from all but a handful of professions, and living in increased poverty. ORT provided education and training in practical occupations like handicrafts and agricultural skills that would help people to help themselves. After the First World War, ORT's headquarters moved to Berlin, and soon it was functioning in many countries. Just as Dad's agronomy studies provided him with the knowledge and skills to stay employed in work he liked throughout his life, so ORT gave my mother the skills to have a viable profession throughout hers.

After his starting work at Poldrob, they decided to get married, and three weeks later, they eloped. Dad's parents didn't want him to marry her because by that time her parents were poor and there was no dowry. His starting salary was 275 złoty a month, not much, but enough to live modestly, and yet his parents insisted they live with them.

Their wedding was simple. One Wednesday Mom said, don't you think it is about time to be married, now that you have a job and tomorrow is

Ascension? So he asked his friend Adek Levin to be witness. Estusia was the other witness.

On Thursday 26 May 1938, they went to an inexpensive rabbi on Graniczna Street. They needed two male witnesses but they had only one. So Dad went out and found another. He was a porter, one of those who carried a platform on his back, tied to his shoulders on which he carried his loads. They delivered all over Warsaw. They were usually Jews, forty years old or more, and they were called camels. So it was a camel that Dad found to be their second male witness. He was small but well built, had red hair and beard, and agreed to take part in the ceremony for five złoty. Dad wrote that "After we left the ceremony my bride and I quarreled. I do not remember why."

Agronomist

Although his work at Poldrob wasn't the work he wanted, it was steady, and the atmosphere was pleasant. They had Dad working in an office, in charge of personnel and checking invoices. Sometimes he would be checking invoices into the night. But he always disliked office work and no matter what the weather, he preferred to be outdoors.

The company shipped hams, pickles, chicken breasts, and more to the U.S., South Africa, and Western Europe. They also had a chicken farm with 750,000 chickens. These would be fed special nourishing food for a few weeks before being slaughtered and canned for export. Once when the farm manager was away for a month's vacation, Dad took over, and he would have twelve scrambled eggs for lunch every day. This farm also exported live chickens, mostly to Italy. Everyone at the farm wanted to be the one to travel with the chickens on the train where they had to be fed along the way. The trip took a few days and in that time the caretaker could collect the hundreds of eggs that were being laid, and then sell them and pocket the money.

He made some new friends at work. Henryk Greenberg, a young man with no schooling, was the chief mechanic. He was a gifted mechanic who had learned his skill from his father. And he rode a BSA 500 cc motorcycle – the most powerful in those days. He was in the army reserves and a real patriot. Eva Rosenfeld, who had a law degree, was the manager of that chicken farm. Hela Rosenberg was a nice girl who worked in the office. Hela and Eva were both in love with Henryk. When the group would go out to the countryside, they would take the company truck, but Hela and Eva would fight for the back seat of Henryk's motorcycle.

Late one night when he was already in bed, Dad got a call from the boss, asking him to come immediately to the office. He had been working there for three months and they wanted to send him to Miława, over 200 kilometers away, to buy cattle. Because it had been a dry year, the peasants in that region did not have enough food for the cattle, and the Department of Agriculture asked the firm to help the farmers by buying off the animals. It was Dad's first chance to show what he could do.

They gave him 300,000 złoty in cash in two small bags that they attached to his arms under his shirt. He was told to take a taxi to the station and catch the train that left in one hour. The next morning he was met in the stock yards near the railroad by a delegate from the regional department of agriculture and a veterinarian.

He started to select the animals, and before dark he had contracted enough cattle for the twenty designated cattle cars that would take them to Warsaw. His superiors had told him to invite the two men out to a restaurant for supper at the hotel. But before that, many of the farmers treated him to a selection of homemade vodka, so by evening he was a little bit loaded.

That day, he hadn't stopped for lunch, and at supper he drank some more, this time black coffee with cognac and then cognac without the coffee. After that, he went up to his room to pay the farmers in cash. That took until 2:00 a.m.

The next day there was double the number of cattle and the same the third day. He called his office to tell them he would be short of money and the next morning a special envoy brought an additional 500,000 złoty. It took three weeks for him to finish.

On the fifth day, the official and the vet suggested they play poker after paying off the farmers. That was at 2:30 a.m., but his boss had told him to accommodate the men as much as possible, besides, he had poker experience from all those days when he had played hooky from high school.

They started to play every night with Dad using company money since he had no cash of his own. After two weeks he had lost 350 złoty. He decided he had to win back that money and he did it in two days. After that he excused himself from any more poker games.

His buying trip was a success, the company was pleased, and he became a cattle buyer with the added responsibility of managing the procedures in the slaughterhouse. After a while he became a pig buyer, and his income went up considerably because in addition to a raise, it was customary for the suppliers to pay the buyer a 10% tip. In a short time, Dad's income went from 350 złoty to 1000 złoty, which was very good money at that time.

Abram was doing well again with his business, and Sonia had started going out again to cafes with her girlfriends. It was 1938. Dad was involved in his work and indifferent to politics, so Hitler's Anschluss went almost unnoticed. But then the Bank Rolny, the Bank of Agriculture in Warsaw, suddenly stopped all credit to the company. A company that did three and a half million złoty worth of business a year can't operate without credit, and Poldrob Ceglana declared bankruptcy late that spring. The workers and the owners were devastated. He had worked for Poldrob Ceglana for two and a half years. Another chapter in his life had closed.

Back to School

Dad felt empty and lost for weeks. He started to read the newspapers and finally realized the danger that Nazi Germany was to the Jews, to Poland, and to the civilized world. He became interested in domestic and international politics.

He decided to finish his agricultural studies but Algeria was too far away and there was no way there to earn extra income, so he decided on the Agriculture Department of the University of Nancy. His parents agreed to help him financially if needed and gave him their moral support as did my mother, who remained in Warsaw with his parents.

Arriving in Nancy in late August 1938, he rented a room close to the Place Stanislas. During his seven months in Nancy, he became friends with a student named Radjoaharisson from Madagascar, attending courses and studying together. One day during a field class, one student of the de la Roche fascists made a nasty remark about his friend being from the French colonies and about both of them being homosexuals. Dad was never one to run away from a fight, even when he was old, and at that time he was only 26. He went over to the guy and his entourage, in front of everyone, students and the professor, and told him he would be waiting for him at the university gym at 8:00 a.m. the next morning. The young fascist never showed up. He was also absent from classes for the next three weeks then, one morning, he showed up, came over to Radjoaharrison and Dad, apologized and offered his hand.

Together with two partners, Dad bought a used 200cc motorcycle and they shared the bike, thus giving him opportunities to see some of the surrounding country. Once, during a holiday, he went with one of the female students to Mulhouse, a three-hour ride, to visit her family. In the Vosges Mountains, it started to rain, then to pour. She was wearing a light summer dress and he was in short sleeves. On what seemed an endless ride, they were pelted with rain, each drop like the prick of a needle.

During his seven months in Nancy, important world events occurred: the Congress of the Nazis at Nuremberg, Hitler's ultimatum to Benesh of Czechoslovakia, and the signing of the accord with Mussolini in December, just before Christmas. But when Germany marched into Czechoslovakia in March 1939, Dad knew he could no longer study. He was three months short of finishing his degree, but he left and returned to Warsaw. Only his family knew that he had left his studies unfinished.

Dad was not alone in deciding to return home. Eighty percent of the Polish students did the same. One of them was a Polish girl from Łódź, who asked him to take her to Strasbourg so she could get an exit visa. After obtaining the visa and visiting the historical city, they realized that it was too late to return to Nancy so they went to a hotel. He assumed they would take two rooms, but she insisted that one room with two beds would save money. She went to bed first while he turned his back. When he went to bed he fell asleep immediately. During the night he felt someone entering his bed. When he turned on the light, there she was. He explained that he was married and could not be involved in such a thing – that even a short romance went against his approach to marriage. She could not convince him otherwise. The next day they rode in silence back to Nancy, with one stop for coffee along the way.

Home Again

In Warsaw, the political scene was throbbing and Dad was in a stormy frame of mind. His parents suggested he take my mother for a vacation, but he refused since he was not working and all his money was gone. But his parents insisted and in July they went with four friends to Czarny Dunajec, south of Kraków, at the foothills of the Tatra Mountains. It was his first time there. Together with Eva and Hela (at peace with each other, Henryk was at his post with the army), Paweł Lewkowicz, a medical student and his girlfriend, they spent a month, using boats, horses with buggies, and taxis to explore the spa town of Szczawnica, the winter sports center Zakopane, and Morskie Oko, the largest lake in the Tatra Mountains that my Dad said is a miniature Lake Tahoe. Dad read the newspaper but avoided talking about the international situation with his friends, wanting to maintain a vacation atmosphere.

Once back, Dad looked for work unsuccessfully for five weeks until he received the call for military duty. Because of his education, he was to be sent to an officers' training school. But the government didn't want too many Jewish officers, so instead they put him in the reserves, having to serve two weeks each year doing pick and shovel work. He didn't mind; he always liked manual labor. Instead of giving them cool water to drink they gave them hot water with mint which he really liked.

He reported to duty on 28 August and started three days of loading sanitary supplies onto railroad cars. On the fourth day, at 5:30 in the morning, he heard the sound of bombs. He couldn't believe it was actual bombardment, and went back to sleep. But the sound didn't stop and he couldn't sleep, so he turned on the radio and found Stefan Starzyński, the President of Warsaw, speaking. It was 1 September 1939 and they were at war. The German army was attacking along the German Polish border; the Luftwaffe was bombing all centers of communication as well as the capital.

Eloped, May 1938

War

Warsaw

When the Germans began bombing Warsaw on 1 September 1939, my father, who had been working in the reserves loading sanitary supplies onto railroad cars, decided to return to his duties in spite of the bombs. When he arrived, he found that about half the people who had been working there were missing. After an hour of loading supplies, the senior officer, a colonel, called him into his office.

He told him the war was lost. They had no defense against the German Luftwaffe, they had inadequate arms, and their famous cavalry with their lances and bravery could not do much against the German Panzer division. And to top it off, their allies France and England had disappeared. He said he chose to talk to Dad because he could see that he could be trusted.

The colonel handed Dad a heavy valise and an envelope and gave him a lady's name and address. He was to deliver the two items to her immediately. He also told him not to return to duty but instead, he said "If you have dear ones, take them and go east by any means, even on foot." Dad took the valise and started walking.

While they had been talking, the train that was being loaded had started to pull out onto the Cross-City Bridge. Dad had just passed the gate when the train was bombed. He stopped for a moment to cry, for the second time in his life, then continued on with his mission and went home.

Dad told his father what the colonel had said, but his father thought he should wait and see how things developed. He was put in charge of the civil defense of his street, but was given no tools. So he called together the ten others whom he was leading and, with bombs falling all around them, sent them out to find some. He got a tip that there was a civil engineer nearby and found the man who gave him some hatchets. They were soon to come in handy.

The family was living at Leszno 56. The next building at 58 was the *Pogotowie Ratunkowe*, or Emergency Medical Services and facing them was *Sąd Grodzki*, the beautiful newly built municipal court building at Leszno 53-55. At about 9:00 p.m. a bomb hit the emergency services building. They could hear and feel the tremendous impact. He went out to check on the situation and his helpers appeared. His building was intact, but next door, the three-story emergency services building was on fire with the employees fleeing for their lives.

There were four ambulances and a few cars parked on the ground floor, but none of them had keys to start the ignition, so they started pushing them out. He had two men break the pavement and formed a line of men who dug dirt that they put into buckets and passed on, through the entrance, up the stairs, and up to the attic to put out the fire. They had no water, that had been previously cut off by the Germans. He sent some men into rooms on the top floor in order for them to throw anything flammable, including furniture, out the windows. Among the men fighting the fire on the roof was Kuba, Mom's brother. Their family's building had already been destroyed.

President Starzyński made radio broadcasts every day, calling on everyone, including women and children, to defend the capital. He refused to leave Warsaw together with other state authorities and diplomats on 4 September 1939. Instead he joined the army as an infantry major. During the Siege of Warsaw, from 8 to 28 September, he commanded the distribution of food, water, and supplies, as well as fire brigades. He also organized shelter for the refugees who came from other parts of Poland and those in Warsaw whose houses were destroyed. But it was his daily radio speeches that kept the military and the civilian population's morale high. Even before the Siege ended, he became the symbol of the defense of Warsaw. He was killed by the Germans in December 1939.

By this time, the Kozłowskis had come down to relative safety from the fourth floor. The building that Mom's family lived in had been bombed, so they also had Ignacy, Dora, Estusia, and Kuba living with them. Rena had gone to stay with her fiancée and his family.

On the 4th, Dad was walking the streets, looking for bread, when he ran into his friend Helenka. They started to walk together when all of a sudden someone called out "Jüdin!, Jüdin!," from across the street where a few German soldiers were standing in front of a former mounted police station. He told Helenka not to pay any attention and to keep walking whereas he crossed the street and approached the soldiers. This led to some confusion on their part as they had Helenka in mind, not Dad, who was blond, blue-eyed, muscular, and probably looked more Aryan than they did. But they collected themselves, gave Dad a broom, and ordered him to start sweeping the yard.

After an hour one of them told him to stop and to follow him. All kinds of thoughts went through Dad's head: the guy wanted to kill him in the cellar? maybe he should grab the bayonet hanging from his belt and kill him first? But before he could decide, they were in the cellar where the wonderful aroma of bacon, soup, and bread were mixed together. The soldier served him a big bowl of soup with pieces of meat and bacon, and a few slices from a big loaf of bread. He waited until Dad was finished and then gave him two loaves of bread, told him to follow him to the gate, then told him to take the bread and go home.

On the 5th, a general got on the radio and told the public that all young people not yet mobilized should leave the capital, go east, and that further orders would follow. Dad decided it was time to go, but no one else in the family wanted to leave. His mother said she had left once, lost everything, and didn't want to leave again, looking around at her apartment and her possessions. His father said, given the position of his wife, he couldn't do anything. Besides, the order was only for young people. Abram was 56, and Sonia was 53.

So Dad took Mom and together with two friends, Władek and his wife Eva, they headed east. About fifteen kilometers out of town, they stopped at the house of some peasants where they were invited to sleep on the floor in the house or on straw in the barn. They slept on the floor. Dinner was potatoes, raw salted bacon, black bread, and sour milk.

The next morning, their hosts gave them breakfast, and when it was time to leave, would not accept any payment, so Dad gave the man his silver-trimmed pipe as a thank you, and he accepted it. That day they heard of a new order saying that everyone who had left Warsaw should return immediately to defend the capital. But it was too late; it was already surrounded by Germans. So they continued east where Dad had relatives and family friends.

After about two and a half weeks, they reached a bridge over the Bug River near Breść-Litewski. There were many German soldiers, so they went back about three kilometers to find out from people coming from the east what their chances would be of crossing the river. Although the chances were meager, they decided to go ahead. So they turned around and once again headed east.

Before reaching the river they were stopped by a German motorcycle patrol of five soldiers who asked for their papers. They saw Dad's name,

Rafał Feliks Buszejkin, and thought that was acceptable. Mom's name, Maria Buszejkin was too. And so were the names of their friends. None of them were Jewish names. Then, all of a sudden, one of the German soldiers pointed at Mom and said, "Look at the small one. She's too dark for a Polish girl." So Dad put out his chest, gathered his chutzpah, and retorted, "What do you Germans think? Having this mighty army and air force, that it gives you the right to insult us by calling us Jews?" The Germans laughed, and the four Jewish friends went on towards the Bug River and Russian controlled territory.

When they got back to the bridge, the Germans were ordering Jews to the right, and others to the left. Dad led his group to the left. When he got to the front of the line, he handed over the two passports and they asked where they were going. "Baranowice," he said. "We have family there and the war cut us off." They asked if he had any money. He told them yes, but that he couldn't give them any because he had only 100 złoty and a long journey ahead. They were allowed to pass and walk across the bridge where they immediately found Russian soldiers.

The Russians were friendly, especially because Dad spoke with them in Russian. They showed them an army truck and said they could sit in the back with the others. But Dad and Mom waited for Władek and Eva who showed up after about fifteen minutes. They had given the Germans 200 złoty to get across.

They all got on the truck and rolled off to Białystok where they found a town full of refugees from the west. One day, walking through town on the crowded streets, Dad came face to face with his old school friend Henryk, who used to eat the girls' lunches. He was with his brother-in-law, very elegantly dressed, joking, friendly, and he asked if Dad needed any money because he had plenty. His wife was in Warsaw and he was planning to cross the border to go back to her. Dad had only 100 złoty, but he hadn't forgotten how Henryk had treated Renia and told him that he had plenty too and said goodbye. After the war when Dad was in New York, he learned from Henryk's sister-in-law that he had been caught by the Germans at the border and ordered to dig a ditch where he was shot and buried.

Władek and Eva decided to stay in Białystok, but my parents, having so little money with them, decided they needed to move on to Baranowice, a small town between Białystok and Minsk, where they had family.

It took two days to get there, sometimes in the back of a truck, sometimes walking. When they would climb into a truck, the driver would come out of the cab and ask if they had a watch for sale, eyeing Dad's wristwatch. When they stopped to rest, they would ask the driver if they had one thing or another in Russia, and the answer was always yes, they had a lot of it. Once, as a joke, Dad asked if they had any oranges. "And how!" was the answer. "There is a big, tremendous factory of them." They understood that people had been instructed to answer that they had everything, that everything was wonderful. It was pure propaganda.

Baranowice

When they finally arrived in Baranowice, they went to find Uncle Julian's house. Julian Myszkowski was Sonia's uncle who had had quite a turbulent life filled with all sorts of women. He was the one who had showed up at Dad's house in Warsaw in 1922 after leaving his first wife, went to France to live in Nice on the Riviera, married a countess, returned to Poland, lived for a few years with a peasant, and eventually fell in love with the butcher's wife and married her.

They rang the bell of a decorated old, Victorian-style wooden house. The woman who answered the door, who had once been the butcher's wife, was about 50 years old and had bleached hair. Dad asked to see Julian and explained that he was his nephew. With a big smile, she invited them in and took them through the tremendous living room, down a long passage, and into the master bedroom. There, in a huge bed covered with a thick blanket, sitting against a large pillow, and wearing a turtleneck sweater and a French beret was Uncle Julian.

He was about 72 by then. Holding a pen and writing, he stopped to kiss them both and embraced Dad with his free arm. "This is my wife, Sonia," he said in a colorless voice. "She will show you to your room and prepare something to eat. You will stay with us as long as you wish. I am glad you are here in one piece." And with that he went back to his writing.

The next morning, Dad spent a third of his remaining money to buy some food for the household and then set off to look for work. Things there were at a standstill, but he managed to find a pick and shovel job with the railroad. Before starting, he had left some applications at companies involved in farming and husbandry, and after two weeks he received a letter, in Polish, from the regional office of the Agricultural Administration. They offered him a job managing a seeds laboratory as well as evening work teaching laboratory techniques to twelve girls, to train them for work.

All his life Dad worked outdoors. The one thing he couldn't stand was sitting indoors all day. The job at the lab was sitting indoors all day, but the lab was next door to the Regional Office of Physical Culture, and one day Dad went over to see if he could arrange something. He spoke with the supervisor and told him about his boxing experience. The man said they were looking for a coach so Dad started working there too. Two evenings a week of physical activity, two hours each time, kept him sane. The pay for the sixteen hours a month at the gym paid almost as much as over 200 hours at the lab. Dad understood this as a reflection of the Soviet sense of values.

Grisza Cyrynski was a friend of Dad's parents, a timber merchant who had moved a few years before from Wilno to Baranowice. He had also lived in Moscow when Dad's family did and left at the same time. Dad met him on the street and he practically dragged him by force to meet his family. Learning that Mom was a dressmaker, the same day, unasked, he sent a new sewing machine and electric iron, so that she could start to work. They began to prosper.

After about five months, advisory notices appeared from the police telling refugees who wanted to emigrate anywhere outside the territory that they should register at the police office. Dad had been in touch with his father by mail, and he had received three letters. Abram told him he was doing okay and that he was working, but he didn't say exactly what he was doing. When Dad saw the police notices, he decided to register to return to his parents' home. So they went the same afternoon and packed their things to be ready to leave at any time. They had to wait three months.

Before the police notices had appeared, some friends of theirs had come up with the idea of sending the women back to Warsaw to get some clothes because there was such a shortage in Russian occupied territory. The women were to go with a paid guide. Their friends assured them there was no risk involved because the German guards were very lenient with women, even when they caught them clandestinely crossing the border. One evening they went to their friends' home to make the final plans but during their meeting something told Dad that it was a bad idea. It was as if a voice was speaking to him. Dad stood up and said, "No." "What are you saying?" asked the husband. "I said Marysia is not going and I'm sorry." Dad wouldn't hear of any protests from Mom or the others, he took her by the hand and left. The other women went and never returned. No one knew what happened to them.

One day, Dad's supervisor told him that he was to go to the Radziwiłł estate in Nieśwież to carry out an inventory of all the animals and agricultural machinery. Nieśwież was where Abram had met Sonia, and this was the estate with the huge castle that his mother's family had been so tied to in the past. He knew it from the stories they had told and now it stood before him in all its grandeur, abandoned, but still majestic. He would have liked to see the clocks that his grandfather used to wind and fix, but he didn't go inside, afraid to face the pillage as all the windows were broken.

In any case, his job had to do with the farm, not the castle. So he toured the estate with the estate community composed of peasants who lived there and who had worked on the estate in the past. There were twenty pure bred Holsteins, no horses (no one knew or would say where they had gone), a pack of spaniels that had been used for hunting, and a large monkey in a cage. They told him that no one needed any of the animals and they didn't have food for them. Dad took one of the dogs home with him and named her Lora.

When he would go to the estate, the community would speak with him in Russian. After rescuing the dog, one of them said to the others, in Polish, "They are not all animals, some of them have a heart." They were surprised when Dad started speaking to them in Polish and told them he was a Pole. After hearing that he was not one of the invaders, they invited him to supper where they ate and drank and exchanged ideas, albeit with caution. In the morning they gave him a large basket of eggs to take home.

On his next visit to Nieśwież he found the time to visit the two sisters, Eva and Olga, at their pharmacy. There he learned the sad news that Eva's husband had died a year and a half earlier of lung trouble. They were no longer looking for husbands, they told him with tears in their eyes.

Every time he went to the Radziwiłł estate, returning the empty basket, they would fill it again. And Lora turned out to be a very loveable dog who would lie day and night on the couch, never sleeping in daytime, just always aware of what was going on and watching their every move, as if to say, "Don't send me away from here, please."

One day in spring 1940, Dad came home with three dozen eggs, and they went to bed as usual at about 11:00. At 2:30 in the morning there was loud knocking at the door. It was the NKVD come to deport them. If they wanted to avoid deportation, they could apply for Soviet citizenship. If not, they had to pack up quickly and come with them.

Six weeks before the deportation, Cyrynski had come with a proposition. He had three trucks ready to take all his possessions to Wilno where they could be sold, and from there he had a permit to take his family to China. He invited Dad and Mom to go with them, and said he had already written to Dad's father about it. Although Dad didn't want to do that, he was grateful to the man for being such a true friend.

Dad refused citizenship; Mom said she needed to go to the bathroom. The two police agents followed her to the outhouse and followed her back, all under gunpoint. Then Mom said she had some eggs she needed to boil so they could take them along. Not being aware of how many there were, the police agreed to wait. It took forty-five minutes to boil the three dozen eggs, three at a time, which was all the pot could hold. They had previously given Lora to one of Dad's boxing buddies who was happy to take her.

They were taken in a waiting army truck to the railroad station where they found thousands of people packed into wagons with signs that read "eight horses or forty men." The doors of the cars were wide open and you could see the people packed inside, sometimes whole families. In one of the cars Dad saw a pair of young men who were smiling and looked like they were going on a picnic. Dad liked that attitude and asked that they be put into that car.

The two men were the only people in that wagon. They managed to close the door most of the way so they could select who else would ride with them, and let in two more young couples. The eight of them traveled together, one couple in each corner. The journey took three weeks – three weeks of thinking about the past and wondering about the future. Dad had a small harmonica and they sang and even danced. Dad wasn't too concerned where he wound up, as long as he didn't have to work underground in a mine.

One day, they were given salt herring to eat, but no water. Normally at the Russian train stations you could get boiling water for free. This was called *kipiatok* untranslatable because it was water specially meant for making tea but for that you needed to carry your own teapot.

Mom said that at one stop she found her lipstick at the bottom of her bundle and, always aware of her looks, she started to put some on to cheer herself up. When Dad saw what she was doing, he was surprised at first, and then angry. He took it from her and threw it away, leaving her broken-hearted and wondering if they had lipstick in Siberia.

The train finally stopped at Tavda (Sverdlovsk Obast), a small town and river port in west central Siberia, located on the Tavda river. About a third of the train passengers remained there, while the rest, including Mom and Dad, were loaded onto a ship that headed up the river. That journey took a week. They were on deck rain or shine and their drinking water was hauled up from the river by a can controlled by a string. There were no bathroom facilities. When a woman had to go, she was held by two men and suspended over the river. The men had it easier.

At the end of the week, their travels were over and their Siberian exile was about to begin.

Siberia

Kureniewo

They disembarked in the midst of a beautiful virgin forest of tall, straight pines, and white birches. The ground was covered with edible berries and the wild strawberries were in such abundance that one could eat for ten minutes, sitting in one place.

Walking through the forest, in half a kilometer they came upon a group of twenty horses and their wagons, and a sign that said "*Zapretnaya zona*" or restricted zone. It was a quarantine zone for the sick horses that had an illness that was dangerous to horses and to people.

Their greeting committee consisted of two men, one in an NKVD uniform with a .45-caliber gun on his hip, and the other, a well-fed and jovial chief administrator. Sacharow, the one with the gun, gave them a short speech where he told them they were here to stay forever. He said that he was in charge of their souls, while Gubin, the chief administrator, was in charge of production. He warned them not to touch the horses' noses and if they did, to wash their hands and not touch their eyes or mouth.

They loaded children and belongings onto the wagons and marched six hours until they came to an abandoned village called Kureniewo. This was a village of log cabins along three parallel streets. At one end was a pig sty, at the other a brick workshop. In the center there was a square with a jail consisting of a small cabin with one small window; a small house like all the others with a sign that said Office; and a blacksmith shop. The whole compound was empty.

Kureniewo was originally built by former Austrian refugees who came voluntarily during the Anschluss to what they thought was the Soviet haven, hoping to build a new life. Instead they wound up in Kureniewo making lumber. They were worse off than Dad and his co-inhabitants because when they arrived there was nothing but the beautiful surrounding pines and birches, and they had to build the place from scratch. They left information about themselves written in German on the walls – loud cries for help. They had been evacuated two days before Dad's group arrived, sent to parts unknown.

The cabins were about 40 feet square and the interiors were divided into two equal rooms by logs that were filled in with moss with a Russian stove, or *pechka*, at the center. The Russian stove, like many traditional peasant hearths, was used for cooking, baking, drying or storing food, and heating the home. It was where people would gather and had platforms to sleep on. It is an important part of Russian culture and figures in its fairy tales.

They were free to choose their housemates; there was no policeman to watch them; no one could escape. Where would one go?

Each cabin was to shelter six families. Mom and Dad shared their space with a forty-year-old woman and her eight-year-old daughter whom they had met on the boat. She was a dentist, intelligent, very timid, and seemed broken in spirit. Their other roommates were two brothers Yankel and Aaron, who were in their twenties. In the other half of the house were three couples, one of them named Danziger. They had two days to make their beds, tables, and benches. Straw stuffed into burlap served as mattresses.

There were 500 people at Kureniewo and Dad, being an agronomist, was put in charge of growing the potatoes to feed them and the oats to feed the 96 horses. The main commercial activity was lumbering, and several sections of the surrounding forest had already been cut. He was given a crew of 150 women and children, 37 men, and 17 horses with plows to remove tree stumps and prepare the land for planting in 37 small fields that were scattered throughout the forest. People were paid for their work according to how much they produced and with the money they could buy bread or potatoes in the village store.

The work force also came from other settlements in the area. There was one camp that was for men only, Kureniewo was for families, and two siblings would count as a family. There were deportees like my parents; some people had been detained for two years, some for three; One old veteran took care of the horses and pigs. He had been sentenced to eight years of "re-education," but didn't know what crime he had committed. He was well read, a gentleman, and he and Dad eventually became good friends.

After a few days, Mom started working making woven shoes called *łapcie*. These were made from strips of bast, the layer between the outer bark and the wood of a tree – typically linden, birch, or elm, but here they were probably using birch. These traditionally-made, inexpensive shoes would be put on over a layer of cloth or rags, laced up the leg with string, and worn year round to work. They were used in Russia, Belarus, Ukraine, and Poland, as well as Lithuania, Latvia, Estonia, and Finland as late as the war years.

The climate was good and people were healthy. Maybe because they worked hard and ate little, they all lost weight, shedding unnecessary kilos. One man named Stanislaw Singer was cured of his liver and heart troubles and he was the store manager and did the least physical work. The one great problem was the mosquitoes and tiny flies in the summer. Everyone would come back from work with bloody faces and hands. Some women even became hysterical because of the insects.

Mom's hair was important to her. It was very thick and very long and she wore it in two long braids. She would comb it every day for twenty minutes with cotton and a fine tooth comb. She washed it once every ten weeks and rubbed petroleum into it after each washing to keep it free of lice. She smelled terrible because of the petroleum, but her hair was shiny, healthy, and free of parasites.

Mom was in charge of the cooking for their cabin and had to be particularly careful when using that Russian stove, not to get too close to the flames, given the flammable state of her hair. Cooking was easy in that there wasn't much to cook, and they were always hungry.

Once, the store had some meat bones – a veritable feast. She cooked the bones three times, and every time there was less flavor until the flavor was only a memory. There was no milk and, except for wild berries, they never saw fruit. She overcame her fear of touching nettles and started using them for soup, discovering that they tasted even better than spinach.

People had quotas for how much work they had to accomplish and some started to even exceed that. The Tradunski brothers were two such workers. They had been lumberjacks in Poland and took easily to the task. Bricks were made, and the mechanics would work at night to sharpen and fix their tools for the next day.

Dad had the potatoes planted in an unusual way that slowed initial growth, but increased it later. When Sacharow came with the *raion*, a county committee, to inspect, they were displeased because the plants looked small. Sacharow, showing off his power to the committee, told Dad that if the harvest was poor Dad would have to pull the potatoes out with his teeth. Dad called him an ignoramus, but did so in Polish and under his breath. When it came time to dig the potatoes up, the harvest was so big that they had to send people from some of the other labor camps to help.

After turning in his report, Gubin told Dad to familiarize himself with the horses and pigs, adding that the next day the big boss would be coming with a veterinarian. Dad understood what was cooking. They were going to try to get him to perform veterinary duties. But he also understood, after his time working in Baranowice, that you don't take a job if you don't know how to do it well. His boss there at the laboratory had explained that their population of 2 million people could be divided into three parts: First, the people who had spent time in jail; second, the people who were in jail; and third, the people who would be spending time in jail. I have learned that this was – maybe still is – a common Russian saying. Dad was not trained and had never worked as a vet. Refusing to work as a vet, Dad was sent to the forest to cut timber.

Gubin was more or less a sympathetic character, but Sacharow was not. However, Dad was not afraid of him. He had the courage of a person who has nothing to lose. What could they do to him? Send him to Siberia? In fact, it could be much worse. They could separate Mom and Dad, or they could send him to work in the mines. As time went on, Gubin, who directed his work was pleased with it, as was the raion.

Winter was approaching and they had to build cellars for storing the potatoes. It was a race with the cold and they won. Gubin was radiant; Sacharow looked like he was choking on his pride.

Dad wanted to build greenhouses so they could grow vegetables in the winter and improve their diet. Gubin liked the idea but said it would be impossible to get any glass. Then Dad came up with an idea. Each house had two double-paned windows. They could each contribute one pane and there would be enough for the project. Gubin got permission from the raion and they started. It was already February.

They had a medical clinic run by a male midwife who was often drunk. His cure for everything was aspirin, when he could get it. When Dad came down with rheumatic fever for the second time in his life, he cured himself in three weeks by doing nothing. In the first week of his illness, Mom got written permission from Sacharow and, together with the cobbler, made the 11-kilometer trip to the village to buy a piece of milk. The milk was frozen and she carried it in a cloth. It was a risky walk with plenty of wolves in the forest and no roads. They were inexperienced and didn't know the way, but they accomplished their task.

On all his projects, Dad worked as a foreman. One day he got into an argument with Sacharow, who accused him of favoring the intelligent among them and trying to win prizes. Dad was insulted. He got angry and stormed out of the office, slamming the door behind him and breaking a window. The next morning he didn't go to work, but waited for Sacharow. When he didn't show up by 9:00 a.m., Dad headed off to work. Around noon, Dad was toasting some frozen bread stuck on a stick held over a fire, when all of a sudden four riders appeared. There were three bosses from the county and Sacharow.

They asked him, in a friendly manner, which surprised him, what had happened the day before. He told them about the incident and asked them to relieve him of his foreman duties. He said he would prefer not to have responsibility for anyone but himself. He said he didn't want to be badgered by Sacharow and added that he liked his work but Sacharow was making it impossible. They told him that Gubin was his direct supervisor but if Sacharow came to the job, that he should at least listen to his suggestions. They wanted him to stay on the job and continue with his projects. From that day until the amnesty, Sacharow didn't badger him anymore.

There wasn't much in the way of entertainment, but once Sacharow organized a chorus of Siberian girls from two villages to come and perform. They started with a simple song, and the audience began to clap along to the beat. The girls, taking the clapping as an insult, left the stage. Sacharow and others tried to explain, but to no avail. That was the first and last of their cultural entertainments.

For the most part, people were too tired in the evenings for distractions and the one day a week they had free they used to cut down trees for firewood. But some played poker. They had no coins and no chips, so one guy had the bright idea of using buttons. The result was that many of the men could no longer close their flies and had difficulty holding up their pants when they worked.

People would often get lost in the taiga when they went out to gather berries or mushrooms, and a posse would be sent out. Most of the time, they were only half a mile away. All the news they had of the outside world came in Pravda, completely controlled by the Soviet government, which Dad described as the only newspaper good for rolling cigarettes.

Mom and Dad adopted a chicken and named her Poulka. They traded some old clothes for her in a native village, and when it was cold she lived inside with them and was part of the family. She laid one or two eggs a week in season and would wait a block from their house to greet them when they came home from work, then would run after them clucking.

One day a parcel arrived for Dad from America – Brooklyn. It was from his uncle Max Rubinson, who was married to Abram's sister Fania. Max had left Russia with nothing at the turn of the century and had become a wealthy man in New York. He married Fania, who was also his niece. When Mom and Dad got married, they had sent Max and Fania their wedding photo. That was to be the only photo of the two of them to survive the war. When Dad left Warsaw in 1939, Abram had given him Max's address and told him to memorize it, and at some point Dad wrote to him.

Besides the overwhelming emotion brought on by the knowledge that there were people out there who remembered and cared about them, there was a veritable treasure inside: four three-meter lengths of the finest wool. This was worth a fortune and once Mom sewed it up, it would be worth even more.

The first of May was a big holiday in the Soviet Union, and part of the celebration was that there was candy and cologne in the store for everyone. They both smelled alike: sweet and flowery. Russian men, used to drinking vodka and unable to get any, would drink anything with alcohol in it, including the May Day cologne. Between the aroma of the candy, and the cologne on their breaths, the men smelled even better than the women.

Dad's four months as a lumberjack served him well later when he was working as a gardener in Los Angeles. He had to remove his first big tree in Glendale, and the neighbors were saying "One man with no power tools doing a job of five people!" "He's a Siberian," the property owners replied.

Amnesty

In late fall of 1942, at 10:00 one morning, everyone was dismissed from work and called to the central square where, mounted on a stage were Sacharow, Gubin, one civilian, and two high NKVD officers. They were told that amnesty had been granted to all of them and they were free to go to any part of the Soviet Union with a few exceptions that were marked in the circular they were given. They did not have to return to work and were to form a line to receive their amnesty certificates. It was music to their ears, and the response was overwhelming. People started singing and dancing in the street.

While standing in line someone touched Dad on his arm from behind. When he turned to see who it was, he found Sacharow with a disturbed look on his face. He told Dad that the hay that had been cut for winter the day before was ready to be collected but he had no one to help him do the work and if the work wasn't done, he would be going to prison since he was the one in charge of it. He asked if Dad could find ten men to help him.

Dad asked around but could not find one man willing to help Sacharow. He felt that helping was the right thing to do and in a way would teach Sacharow a lesson in human values. In the end he found nine boys, aged fourteen to nineteen, who agreed to come and Sacharow also showed up after a while in his pants and shirt but no uniform and no gun at his hip. They all worked together and before sundown they were finished. Sacharow turned around and, without saying a word, took the path to the village and vanished among the trees.

The evacuation began the next day. Dad loaded eighteen sacks of potatoes and twelve sacks of carrots onto a wagon, and the same horses that had brought them in would now take them to their so-called freedom. In 11 kilometers they came to the village and found a woman they knew named Marusia, who lived alone with her children. Her husband, a simple peasant, had been arrested one night, taken away, and never heard from again. She had told them that probably when he was drunk he had said something he shouldn't have and one of the neighbors reported him to the police. That is how the country was then, everyone was afraid to speak. Fathers feared their sons. You never knew to whom you were speaking – it could be an NKVD agent or informant. Dad and the other deportees weren't afraid because as they saw it, the worst had already happened. They either didn't know or didn't dwell on much harsher punishments given out in the USSR, and they were unaware of what was happening in Poland and throughout Europe under the Nazis.

There was a little Jewish guy named Shaia, who was not afraid. From day one, he had pretended to be crazy. He fooled them all: Sacharow, Gubin, and the raion committee. He would play on words by combining Russian, Polish, and Yiddish to make up amusing or insulting sayings that turned out to be "What kind of country is this where a holiday is an outhouse?" and another, *Kak tvaja familia*?" that in Russian would be "How is your family?" but with one of the words in Yiddish made it "Shit on your family." He got away with saying whatever he liked, was never disciplined, and was even relieved of work.

Dad left six sacks of potatoes and five of carrots with Marusia as a token of their gratitude. With as little as she had, she had sometimes brought food to them and they didn't have anything during that time to repay her with. He saw her as a typical simple Russian person with a good heart. She was a woman alone with children and still had the time and compassion to think of two complete strangers. They embraced, kissed on both cheeks, and left.

When they finally arrived at the Tavda river, there was a steamer waiting for them. This time they were singing onboard until their throats were sore. When they got to the town of Tavda, they waited for a train.

Receiving amnesty papers, you had to declare where you wanted to settle until the end of the war. Dad chose a small town that was not far from three neighboring countries: Iran, Afghanistan, and China, thinking that one day before the war ended, they could cross one of those borders clandestinely and make their escape.

But that was just a dream. A few single men had tried it, were caught, and were sent back to Siberia or to Kazakhstan to work in the mines. The only person Dad had heard of who had succeeded was Milek Gordchowski, the brother of one of Mom's classmates, who later changed his name to Max Hodder, lived in Los Angeles, and worked as a travel agent.

At Sverdlovsk, they took a regular passenger train going to Asia Minor through Omsk, Novosibirsk, Semipalatinsk, passing Lake Baikal, the world's largest freshwater lake by volume, containing more water than all the American Great Lakes combined. It is also the world's deepest and oldest and among the world's clearest lakes.

Tashkent

They got off the train at Tashkent, the capital of Uzbekistan and the most beautiful city they had seen in Russia. Dad called it the city of flowers and pickpockets. They passed through the train station with Dad carrying all his remaining sacks of potatoes and carrots, and they made camp in front of the station, together with hundreds of others who had also come from the north. That part of the country is known for its melons. They were a real treat for people who hadn't seen a piece of fruit in over a year. They ate voraciously and were in heaven until their insides, not used to the joy of eating melon, rebelled, Dad's among them.

Mom started selling the potatoes and carrots on the steps in front of the train station. She would fill a five-gallon bucket and ask twenty rubles for it. In an hour Dad's back-breaking cargo was all sold to the last potato.

Dad went to visit the Ministry of Agriculture to see where he might find a job, and was able to meet with the Vice Minister, a handsome man in his fifties. He had long grey hair, a mustache, and the face of an intellectual. This man gave Dad a referral for a job in Samarkand.

When he got back to the train station he told Mom the good news and, feeling happy and light-hearted, they left their belongings with friends and set off on a streetcar to enjoy the city and see the museum. Tashkent, at least in those days, was known as the City of Thieves and the streetcars were their preferred arena, and so it was that during their ride someone stole Dad's wallet with all his papers from his back pants pocket. This was a real disaster. They had taken their identity papers, Dad's university records, and most important, the papers that said they were Polish citizens,

Mom, in hysterics, screamed to stop the car. She wanted everyone searched. People looked at her as if she was insane. The conductor explained that whoever had taken the wallet was long gone and told them to go to the police. Mom was afraid the police would not believe them and without papers, they could get into trouble. But the conductor assured them they would be believed. Apparently this kind of thing happened so often one more instance would not be questioned.

They were astonished and relieved when the police did believe them, but they said it was unlikely that they would be able to recover the wallet since documents such as those were valuable. So Dad decided he would go back to the Vice Minister who had seen all his papers and ask for his help.

He was not disappointed. The man gave him another copy of the work referral and a letter that identified all the documents he had seen, including the amnesty certificate and noted that it had all been stolen. What he could not do is certify that Dad was a Polish citizen. Only the NKVD could provide that sort of document and for that they would have to return to Swerdlosk.

They had enough money to do it, so they took a train back. In Swerdlosk they went to the NKVD headquarters, an intimidating building that took up a whole square block. While Mom waited outside, Dad went in. He was taken to the office of a captain who had him sit down. When Dad told him his story and showed him his work referral, the man started to shout. He was angry that Dad and maybe all the other refugees were being allowed to travel anywhere they wanted. There is a war on, he said. Transportation is needed for the war, not for you to play tourist. He told Dad that he would verify his Polish citizenship but they were not to go far from Swerdlosk.

Dad agreed and the captain then took him out of the office, which was on the second floor and they went down five floors, deep into the basement where they continued walking. It took ten minutes. Finally he got a ladder, climbed up to get a big, thick, heavy book, and found Dad's name. They went back up the stairs and to a map in his office. Choose where you will settle. Dad had no idea so he put his finger somewhere on the map. Very well, said the captain, and he had his secretary type up the certificate, handed it to Dad, and reminded him that he had given his word of honor to go to Tyumen.

Dad shook his hand and started to leave when the captain stopped him. "Where are you going?" "To the street where my wife is waiting, and then we will take a train to Tyumen." "One does not leave the NKVD building like that. This is not a restaurant. You need a pass." He ordered the pass to be typed up, signed it, and said, "Now you can go." Dad would have run if he could.

As agreed, they went to Tyumen, a small town with a Polish majority of second generation Polish deportees from the 1905 uprising. There he met some friends from Kureniewo. Everyone was depressed. There were no jobs.

They rented a room from the sister of a deceased Polish priest and Dad started looking for work. After three weeks he found a job supervising the collection of agricultural taxes from peasants. He was given 20 horses with wagons and 20 men and was to start on Monday.

Monday came and with it, at 6:00 a.m., came Sacha Gutrieiew – a strange-looking man with curled feet, a big belly, no neck, crossed eyes, red hair and beard. His piercing greenish grey eyes were constantly on the move, inspecting everything. He was about four foot six and weighed well over 200 pounds. Mom found him frightening to look at.

They set off to the first designated cottage to meet their first victim. On the way, Sacha started to explain. "Tovarich, inspector," he began, "You and your wife have to live like my family. I was doing better before, working in Moscow as an animal-catcher for a shelter. I caught dogs and cats. Some of them went to the shelter; some went to private customers until they caught me and sent me here. But here is the same story. Nobody can live from the wages they pay, so we steal. But we are clever and very careful. For example, we take in ten sacks of rye with a total weight of one ton, and before we deliver it we take one third and blame the loss on the heat and humidity and loading and transport. We deliver two-thirds of the total and the rest we sell on the black market. We'll divide the money in two parts: one for you and one for me. If you don't like this proposition, the whole crew will get rid of you. So what do you think?" Dad told him he would give him an answer in a week.

Dad decided to quit that job. The problem was that to refuse work in Russia at that time was impossible. The officials were not pleased but he kept insisting that he was an agronomist and this job didn't call for his skills. They finally agreed to let him go.

He immediately started to look for professional work again, but he was blacklisted so he took a job as a carpenter, making skis. That work consisted of scraping the skis, putting them into an iron frame, and taking then to a hot room heated to 100 degrees Fahrenheit. The room they were working in was 25 degrees Fahrenheit. After three weeks Dad got sick, was feverish and couldn't leave his bed. It took six weeks for him to be able to stand and walk a little. He had had enough. He told Mom that they were leaving. He would go and take that job he had been referred to in Samarkand. In the meantime, Mom had made eight skirts from Max's American wool and had sold six of them at the market for a good price. She had two skirts left for when they would need them, and more than enough money to buy train tickets. One evening they loaded all their possessions on a sled and headed for the railway station.

Hundreds of people were camped out at the station – women on one side, men on the other. To buy tickets you had to get into one of two lines. One was for business travelers, the other was for getting to work. Dad got into the work line. The clerk told him he had to wait; there were other more important people waiting who would go first: high military officers, and high placed civilian officials. Then, all of a sudden the clerk said 340 rubles for two tickets. It was a miracle.

They boarded a train for Tashkent where they would change trains for Samarkand. However, from a group of Poles on the train they learned of a town before Tashkent where there was an organized Polish committee connected to the Polish Embassy in Moscow and the Polish government-in-exile in London. There were 27,000 refugees who were receiving help from abroad, and who had a good social life. They changed their plans.

Kazakhstan

Dzhambul, in Kazakhstan, was a dusty town with unpaved roads and no sidewalks. When the wind blew one could hardly see ten feet ahead. During the rainy season, the mud would be four inches thick and without proper shoes, you would suffer with cold and misery. Happily, the rainy season was very short, just two or three weeks. The soil was unstructured silt, tiny particles that when dried, would form a perfect cloud of dust in the wind or a profound layer of mud in the rain. Immediately after the rain there would be a breathing spell when the earth would form a hard crust which was good to walk on while leaving imprints of what had passed on its surface.

There was no transition between summer and winter, simply an immediate change with no fall in between. There was little vegetation and the town had no trees. Looking down the street you could see in the distance and to the horizon only the flat surface of the steppe covered with dried grass and weeds. The only visual distraction was the snow-capped Tian Shan mountains – the Mountains of God – off in the distance, on the border between Kazakhstan, Kyrgyzstan, and China to the south.

Almost all the homes were built of adobe from the local soil. Straw or cow manure was added to the mud and dried in the sun to make the bricks, thus about twenty percent of the houses dissolved and disappeared in the rainy season.

There were some buildings made of regular bricks that withstood the vagaries of the weather; those were government buildings, schools and a few factories.

It took them two hours to find a place to stay. It was one room at the back of a property with the landlady living in the front, and a well with a wooden frame in the center of the yard, one corner of which was the cow's quarters.

They went to the Polish *placówka*. Placówka means a picket as in soldiers on guard protecting from a sudden attack, but it can also mean an outpost in a distant or unpopulated area, facility, institution, or local headquarters. This placówka was an organization connected to the Polish government-in-exile in London that administered aid to Polish citizens living in the area. They went to register and to see about Dad finding professional work and were told that there was little chance of finding anything with the Russians, who didn't like to hire Poles. The clerk said that everyone made a living buying and selling at the market. A few worked at low-level jobs in order to have a ration card and to steal at the place of work and then sell that at the market. The outlook was gloomy.

He added that Polish institutions provided assistance to the refugees from time to time with care packages of clothing that would arrive from the United States and Britain, and those were distributed among what he referred to as those of "former Polish grandeur."

The clerk was finished but Dad was not. In lieu of assistance with food or clothing, he wanted a letter from the head of the Polish placówka to the Russian authorities requesting that Dad, a Polish citizen, be given a job in the field of agronomy. This he got, signed by Dr. Kinstler (who was also an agronomist and later also lived in Los Angeles) with a wish of good luck. Letter in hand, he headed off to the Regional Offices of the Russian Department of Agriculture.

Kinstler's letter did no good, but the letter from the Uzbek Vice-Minister made an impression. Talks began with the Russian officials about how they might employ Dad.

When Dad met with the raion (county) agronomist who ran the seeds laboratory and the zootechnics (animal husbandry) service, there was another man in the office standing at the back and listening attentively. He was very tall, broad-shouldered, and muscular. His face was broad and open, his eyes were blue and friendly, and he had a nice smile. He extended his hand. "Kosmin," he said.

Kolkhoz

Kosmin was the director of an MTS, (*mashinno-traktornaya stantsiya*, or machine tractor station), a state-owned institution that rented heavy agricultural machinery, such as tractors and combines, to a group of neighboring *kolkhozy* (collective farms) and supplied skilled personnel to operate and repair the equipment. On the spot, he offered Dad a position as master agronomist, managing the agriculture of five kolkhozes.

He asked Dad if he knew how to ride a horse. Of course he did. They liked each other from the first moment and that friendship endured for the next four and a half years.

"Your Russian is perfect," he said. "You'll have to learn some Kazakh." He told Dad to be at the MTS at the north edge of town at 6:00 a.m. the next day.

When he got there at 5:45, Kosmin was already in his office, and he began to familiarize Dad with the extensive requirements of Russian bureaucracy. There were forms for everything. One could hardly make a move or carry out any task without putting it on paper and having it signed.

After two hours they got into a five-ton truck and went to see the 20,000 acres of land and the people that Dad would be working, eating, and sleeping with for the next few years. The kolkhozes Dad was to work with were Craidawa, Kzyl-Dehcan (which means red power in Kazakh), Kujbyshewa, Chaldans, and Sinugrbai. They ranged in distance from Dzhambul from two and a half to fifty kilometers. All but Kujbyshewa were originally Kazakh with a few Uzbeks. Kujbyshewa was almost completely populated with former deportees from 1920-1923. These were Ukrainian peasants who for political reasons were deported to the barren steppes of Kazakhstan to start a new life, far from their homes where their ancestors had plowed the rich black Ukrainian soil.

These collective farms were not really true cooperatives, except for nominal joint ownership of non-land assets by the members. Remuneration had always been in proportion to labor and not from residual profits, which meant that members were treated as employees and not as owners. Membership was not voluntary but was imposed by forced collectivization. Also, members did not have the right of free exit, and those who managed to leave could not take their share of assets with them.

Each kolkhoz had 4,000 acres of arable land, a few hundred communal cows, herds of sheep, and the use of a dozen heavy duty tractors and three or four combines. The main crop was the sugar beets that took up about 90% of their land. Secondary crops included winter wheat, melons, corn, and legumes. The population varied from 350 at Sinugrbai to over 600 at Kujbyshewa.

The first thing Dad noticed as he surveyed the fields with Kosmin was the absence of men doing manual work. The hardest work in the fields was being done by women, and they were working in the hot sun from sunrise to sunset with two hours rest for lunch from 12:00 to 2:00. In the tractor brigade were a few young girls who were very good at their work.

Water was brought by a network of ingenious channels from far away mountains. Supervision, control, and distribution of the water were part of Dad's responsibilities. The work was done by hand, blocking some channels while opening others. This was done with a hoe that weighed fifteen pounds. The hoes used by the women in the fields weighed ten pounds.

After spending about six hours visiting the kolkhozes and being introduced to each chairman, they returned to the MTS station where Kosmin introduced Dad to the mechanics. He also gave him some hints for how to behave with the native Kazakhs: that he sit on the floor with the men rather than the chair that will be offered, and that he eat hot soup or meat with his hands like everyone else, rather than use the plate, knife, and fork he will be given. He said it would be good public relations, and he was right.

The next day Dad mounted his horse, an 11-year-old mare with a wound on her back under the saddle. She was a pacer, one of those horses who, when they walk or trot, throws forward the front and back leg on the same side, then does the same on the other side, like a camel.

The Kazakh farmers had been nomads who had been forced to settle and grow crops 25 years before. But they maintained some of their old customs. They used yurts to sleep in during the hot summers where years ago they would have left for the highlands, but now they had to remain and produce sugar, which they didn't use at all.

They drank koumiss, a fermented beverage, similar to kefir but made from mare's milk that is said to taste like champagne mixed with sour cream. Due to the milk's naturally high sugar content, making kumiss requires nothing but a mare. Mongolian nomads simply churned horse milk in vats, much like butter, until the milk acidified and yeasts produced alcoholic carbonation. Because mare's milk contains more sugars than cow's or goat's milk, when fermented, koumiss has a higher, though still mild alcohol content compared to kefir. The liquid is cultured to make it drinkable. Unlike cow's or yak's milk, mare's milk contains so much lactose that it has a severe laxative effect. Kazakhs like to say that koumiss makes your eyes sharper, your feet stronger and your soul younger. Around 1250, explorer William of Rubruck journeyed across the steppes and raved about the drink, stating that "Koumiss makes the inner man most joyful." The alcohol content of koumiss is about 2.5%, less than the average beer, but Dad didn't realize there was any alcohol.

One day he had a mid-day meal of two pints of koumiss and two pieces of *lepyoshka*. This is a Central Asian naan that originates in Uzbekistan. It can be made plain, with just flour, yeast, and salt, or it can also incorporate butter, sesame seeds, lamb fat, different kinds of meats and nuts, or even raisins. After the meal, Dad got on his horse, galloped 12 miles to the next site, and arrived with a terrible headache. When he told the water mill manager about his headache the man laughed and explained that when you drink koumiss, you have to wait an hour before riding.

Winter homes on the kolkhozes were built with bricks made of mud mixed with cow dung. They also made briquettes for heating fuel from the dung; these were called *kizyak*. The kizyak are still being used in some rural communities in Uzbekistan that are not yet connected to the gas grid and they are still made in the same way, mixing the dung with water and wheat stubble. Making the kizyak was (and still is) women's work. In order to prevent kizyak theft by unscrupulous neighbors, each housewife left her mark in the briquette while it was still moist.

There was resentment on the part of the kolkhoz leaders because the Russians in charge did not speak Kazakh and the Kazakhs spoke only limited Russian. After six months, Dad surprised Kosmin by learning to speak passable Kazakh.

The kolkhoz VIPs were all party members, but the indoctrination didn't seem to have soaked in. One day Dad was riding with six of the leaders from one of the kolkhozes when the others asked Dad to ride ahead and they would catch up. Dad rode slowly and when he turned to see what they were up to, he saw them all down on their knees, bowing in front of the ruins of a building.

When the yurt became too hot they slept out under the sky with a *korpeshe*, a down bag used by nomads that served as both mattress and cover and used a saddle as a pillow. It never rained in the summer and the nights were warm and beautiful. At Sinugrbai, the chairman's goat would get up at 5:00 a.m. and start eating Dad's hair. This always happened when he slept there. The chairman's family laughed and said that was why Dad was getting bald.

One day at Kujbyshewa, when he was working on papers with the secretary, the chairman and caretaker came in. They pointed to his head and then to the photo of Comrade Lenin that was hanging on the wall and said, "You, tovarich, must be very smart like Lenin who was bald." Dad responded, "And how about tovarich Stalin?" A confused silence overtook the room.

His schedule and lifestyle was the same as the native people that he worked among. In the summer he would get up at 5:30, wash his eyes and gargle with water, drink a quart or two of koumiss, and eat a piece of lepyoshka. Then he would saddle up his mare and go out into the fields.

Lunch was at noon, the same food they had at breakfast. Then they would sleep for an hour, and from 2:00 to 7:00 p.m. he would do paperwork in the office. Supper with the chairman was from 11:00 p.m. to 1:00 a.m. That was the only big meal and took at least an hour to eat. The men would sit in the first row around the fire in the center of the yurt. Dad would be seated next to the man of the house who took a large leg of mutton from the iron pot of steaming soup, take a few bites, and then pass it to Dad who would do the same and hand it to his neighbor. After it was passed around the first row, the leg went to the second row where the women and children would be standing. The soup would be eaten with their hands. It took a while to learn how to do this, and it took time for the initial burns to heal. When the men were finished, the women would come with water for them to rinse their hands. But the supper wasn't yet over.

Alcohol is regarded as the glue of friendship in Kazakhstan. Toasts are features of big events and declining a drink is considered rude. An evening is not considered complete until many bottles have been finished. In Dad's time, when the men were finished eating, and had rinsed their hands, they would bring out a couple of bottles of a bluish alcohol. This must have been vodka as it is the most popular and ubiquitous of alcoholic drinks in Kazakhstan. Once that was consumed, it was 2:00 a.m. and off to bed.

Summer nights were spent outdoors sleeping under the stars. Dad found it to be a blessing because the yurts were full of lice. The beds, bedding, everything. The whole place was swarming; the whole yurt seemed to move. So being outdoors was an escape.

Dad would work five days a week and then go home to Dzhambul. He would wash before going in and would enter naked as a final precaution. But he brought lice with him anyway and consequently, he got typhoid fever in 1944.

Work was more difficult than it might have been for the lack of spare parts. During the war, all resources were concentrated on the war effort. The back country had to patch things up as best they could. All they had at their disposal was the ingenuity of the mechanics to devise what was needed so people could work, and for the most part, people had to rely on themselves.

Unofficial exchanges were forbidden by law. One day Kosmin sent Dad to Frunze (now Bishkek), capital of Kyrgyzstan, about 300 kilometers from Dzhambul and once on the Silk Road. Bishkek is situated at an altitude of about 800 meters (2,600 feet), just off the northern fringe of the Kyrgyz Ala-Too Range, an extension of the Tian Shan mountain range. These mountains rise to a height of 4,895 meters (16,060 feet). North of the city, a fertile and gently undulating steppe extends far north into neighboring Kazakhstan.

The reason for the trip had to do with melons. Dad had twenty acres of melons in each kolkhoz and one day when he was inspecting, he found the first sign of bacterial disease. He would need flowers of sulfur to spray, but they didn't have any.

Kosmin had a friend who was a director of an MTS in Frunze, and he needed potatoes. So Kosmin arranged for fifteen sacks of potatoes for Frunze, and two sacks for the station master where Dad and the potatoes would be catching a train the next day.

Kosmin reminded him that this was a "diplomatic mission and has to be done in complete secrecy. If anything goes wrong we could all go to jail." And so it was, in order to save government melons, the four of them were risking arrest and prison even though no flowers of sulfur could be acquired through regular channels. The next day Dad went to Frunze and happily accomplished his mission. The melons were saved.

The Caucasians

At the beginning of 1943, Dad received a group of transplants from northern Caucasus. These were the Karachays and the Chechens. Although they lived not far from each other in the beautiful high mountains of the northern Caucasus, everything about them was different. First of all, they spoke different languages. Physically, the Karachays were typical mountain people: tall, robust, with straight black hair, black or blue eyes, and they were friendly, smiling at their misery of being deported from their snowy mountains where the air was fresh all year around to the barren steppes of Kazakhstan where the temperature in summer was 100 degrees. The Karachays did not like the Chechens who they said were the only people in the northern Caucasus that did not mix with the others and had a language that nobody understood.

The Chechens were a proud people, and their posture, actions, and behavior at work were marked with dignity. They wore their traditional clothes that included a *chokha*, a woolen coat with a high neck; *gazyrs*, implements to hold rifle charge, worn on each side of the breast to enable the horseman to load a gun while on the move; and a *kinzhal*, a curved, double edged dagger, the traditional dagger of the Caucasian equestrian tribes and the Cossacks, worn on their belt. The authorities did not dare to take away those daggers. In 2017, the Kinzhal hypersonic, air-launched ballistic missile, named for the dagger, was unveiled by President Putin. The Chechen deportation occurred right after the Red Army reconquered the territories occupied by the German army, when the Stalinist regime accused the Chechens of massive collaboration with the German invaders and then deported them en masse.

One kolkhoz had two big empty barns and that is where the new arrivals from the Caucasus were put – each group in its own barn. The first few days they spent fixing up the old barns, and then they started to die. Six hundred had arrived, and within two weeks, 150 had died. Dad arranged for a Polish refugee doctor to come from Dzhambul. She was saddle-sore when she arrived, not being used to travel by horseback, but her diagnosis was quick. It was typhoid fever.

Dad organized all the horses and wagons that were not being used, loaded everyone with their possessions, and took them to Kujbyshewa, the only kolkhoz that had two big Russian baths. Everyone and everything was steamed. There were a few more deaths but then the epidemic stopped. Afterwards, when Dad would visit them, he would be embarrassed when they fell to their knees and started to pray for his health. Dad had new friends.

He gave them some oats and showed them where to plant, and also provided water, all kept a secret from the Soviet authorities. They had a good yield from the oats they planted and this enabled them to stave off hunger with some extra to sell or trade on the black market.

The Caucasians became an asset to the kolkhoz. They were good workers and intelligent people. Dad hoped that they would be able to return to their beautiful high mountains after the war.

After the general wheat harvest, Dad organized, probably the first-ever, track and field competition between the Karachays, the Chechens, and the Kazakhs. For a shotput they used an eight-pound rock, for a javelin they used a spade, and so on. Everyone had a lot of fun.

When the time came for Dad to leave Kazakhstan in April 1946, a delegation of the Caucasians came to their flat in Dzhambul, bringing presents: a kinzhal for Dad, and a smaller one for Mom plus some wool for her to knit with. The two daggers were made from a broken tooth of a tractor rake, the handles were wood, and the decoration on the handles was made from pieces of glass and broken combs.

Crime and Punishment

Crime and punishment was a Soviet feature at least as much as it had been an imperial one. There was the young tractor driver who got drunk at his wedding. The next morning he overslept and went late to sow the fields that had been prepared. The delay meant that the seeds were sown onto dry soil and they didn't germinate. An NKVD agent came to investigate. Dad, being in charge of the agriculture on the kolkhoz had a conversation with him and explained how they only had four people to farm over 2000 hectares (almost 5000 acres) and it was impossible to be everywhere at once. The inspector told him "Nothing is impossible in the Soviet Union," warned him to be careful, and left. Dad never said anything about the young tractor driver who could have been punished with five years of hard labor.

Elders from the Caucasian community told Dad that not only were they not receiving their allotment of milk, they were receiving almost no milk at all and there wasn't enough even for children and those who were ill. Dad went to have a talk with Shoura, the German woman in charge of the milking and she told him she gave all the milk to the Caucasians except for one glass that she kept for her daughter.

Dad was sure she was lying, so he went one morning at 4:30 to wait in the barn. There he saw her loading most of the milk onto wagons full of melons that were going to market. She cried when he confronted her, promised never to do it again, and Dad never reported her.

One day the Caucasians told him that their bread was beginning to be full of dirt or sand. Dad didn't think it was Shoura again after the milk incident, but dirt was being mixed into the flour that was being distributed from Shoura's store. There was only one other person who could be doing it.

Early one morning Dad hid again and watched as they unloaded the wagons bringing groceries to the store. Once they had unloaded and were returning to the city, Dad caught up with them and found two one-hundred kilo sacks of flour. He told them to return to the store and unload the flour. There Shoura's helper jumped on Dad, but Dad gave him a punch and stopped him in his tracks, made him get his things and leave. He would have been given five years or more of prison, but Dad's only concern was to protect the rights of the Caucasian community who could not defend themselves because when they complained, no one listened.

There were people from outside who would bring horses in at night to graze in a field growing grain meant for winter feed for the horses of the kolkhoz. There were two kolkhoz directors who spirited off two five-ton trucks of watermelons one night. There were two other officials who, in order to survive the winter, wanted to plant extra fields of wheat and sugar cane without the government knowing. They wanted Dad to provide the water and offered to give him 25% of the total yield. The fields were far from the city and the chance of discovery was small. Dad did his part but refused any pay. The scheme was never discovered.

After about two years Kosmin sent Dad to Alma-Ata (now Almaty), then the Kazakhstan capital, to take a course in wheat grain analysis. Dad said he knew the subject, but Kosmin said it was required by law. Dad was there for three days, took the course, passed the exam, and received a certificate.

When he got back he had a surprise waiting for him. At the corral there was a *tabun*, or herd of wild horses from China. He had his choice and could replace his old mare. He picked a beautiful four-year-old black stallion that had never been ridden. Dad knew how to ride a horse, but he didn't know how to break one in, but an old Mordvin helped. He was a hot-blooded horse with a skimpy tail and turned out to be the fastest horse in the region.

Once a year, the Kazakhs would play *kokpar*, an old game played by nomadic tribes. Often played on a field with goals, here the carcass of a decapitated goat would be placed out in the steppe and the players would try to bring it to their yurt.

First prize was the only prize. This game has been described as blood-drenched polo with the headless goat as the ball, or the symbiosis of rugby and horse riding.

If you asked a player, which is more important, the horse or the rider, they would tell you the horse. And thus, many players asked Dad if he would lend them Blackie. He would let each one of them try to ride him, but Blackie would have no one but Dad. And when they had races, no one could beat him.

Dad took an additional job at the state leather factory and had another source of income. He got two pair of boots and five kilograms of buckwheat. It was a big event; no one had seen buckwheat in years. Mom invited as many people as they could fit in the room, and among others who came were Mannes and Fela Krakowski. Fela had washed Mannes's only white shirt shortly before the event and had hung it out to dry. But it didn't dry completely and poor Mannes came wearing a damp shirt. Mannes and Fela became good friends with my parents. They later met again in the United States where Mannes and Dad became business partners, and their two children, Jerry and Hannah (Honey to us) became like cousins to me. But that day, Mannes ate his buckwheat kasha in a soggy shirt.

Mom busied herself making embroidered jackets from strips of fur and sold them for a profit. She also taught other women how to make them. The skills she had learned at ORT never let her down.

In 1944, with Soviet permission, the Polish First Army (also known as Berling's Army) was being formed and Dad decided to join them. He bought a ticket at the train station, but after a few hours of waiting it was announced that the train wouldn't arrive for another 24 hours because the bridge at Alma-Ata had been washed away by torrential waters.

Dad went back home and woke the next morning with what he thought was a cold but after five days was diagnosed as typhoid fever. He was taken to a hospital by horse and buggy and put into the typhoid ward with 26 other patients. All the men were delirious.

The occupants in the bed to his right changed five times in the six weeks that he was there. None of them had survived. Each one, knowing he was dying, would ask Dad to give something they were leaving behind – things of no value except to that person and probably the recipient – to a wife or daughter or friend. They would leave those objects on the night table between their beds. When he finally left the hospital, he had a small collection of these souvenirs but no idea to whom they once belonged or to whom they should be given.

While Dad had been sick, the food supply at home had been reduced to bread only. When he was working, he would bring home sour cream, butter, eggs, meat, all presents from his Kazakh friends. He told my mother to go to the Placówka, explain her situation, and ask for help, and this she did. Three weeks after he left the hospital, a delegate came to find out what type of help they needed. Dad told him they didn't need help anymore. They had needed it when he was ill in the hospital, but not now. A few days later he received a letter from Dr Kotas, asking him to come to his office. There, he was asked to sit. Dr. Kotas left and came back with all the employees of the organization and told them to honor my father as an example of patriotism. At first Dad didn't know what it was all about. Then Dr. Kotas explained that in the three years of the organization's existence, no one had ever refused help before.

Kotas asked Dad if he would supervise the distribution of goods to the Polish community in the local kolkhozes. Dad accepted but when he found there were a lot of irregularities and stealing, he resigned.

But there were many good people among the Russian peasants and common people. Their landlords, Maksim and Shura had very little but were generous. When Dad first started to work for the MTS and they had almost nothing to eat because he wasn't yet bringing food from the kolkhozes, one evening the curtain separating the two rooms were drawn aside and Shura appeared with half of a cooked sugar beet on a plate. The other half she kept for her family for their supper. Shura, and Marusia, the woman in Siberia with the children but no husband, and others, were people

Dad never forgot. He said you can say whatever you think about the Soviet regime, but nothing bad about the Russian people who are full of heart.

It was common for the men in the kolkhozes to practice bigamy. They would refer to these women as "cousins." One night, Amalf, chairman of a kolkhoz, sent Dad one of his cousins. Dad was sound asleep when he suddenly felt someone by his side. He got up, went to his host's bed, and asked him to explain.

The man broke out swearing in Russian and Kazakh, digging up long-forgotten words, insulting him and complaining about ingratitude. It took Dad some time to explain that he was as religious as he was, but in his religion it was forbidden to sleep with more than one wife. "Strange religion. Your nation must be very poor and with very few children," he replied. Dad told him he was right, and that satisfied him. He ordered the woman out of the bed and proposed a drink of their unpurified alcohol. Dad couldn't refuse again, so they drank for a couple of hours, while Dad answered his questions about Poland and about drinking. He liked all that he heard except the bit about monogamy.

Dad noticed that sometimes women in the fields would hide their laughter as he passed by. Once, when the chairman of another kolkhoz was taken into the army, his wife, who became acting chairman, made an attempt on his marital vows. But Dad would not be swayed, the attempt came to nothing, and Dad made sure not to sleep in her yurt again.

When the head of the Placówka changed, the new man, former judge Muttermilch from Warsaw, came to speak with Dad. He said he was surrounded by corrupt employees, a big part of the goods failed to be distributed because they went to the black market, and he asked Dad if he would accept a job of overseeing the distribution.

Dad was happy with his agricultural work at the MTS and didn't want to change jobs. But he was beset by Mom and many of their acquaintances to take the job. Cleaning up the corruption would mean more aid for everyone. The pressure went on for weeks until he finally decided to take the new job. Kosmin agreed but would not release Dad from his job for another ten weeks, until the sugar beets were treated for blight. When the work was done, he hugged Dad with all his might, kissed him on both cheeks, and told him if anything went wrong, he would be welcome back.

Dad's first job with the Placówka was to register all the 27,000 Polish citizens in that region. That included the city of Dzhambul and 37 kolkhozes, and he did it all on foot. It took him three weeks to meet all the Polish people, from new born babies to 80-year-old grandmothers. He called it his "long march." This gave the Placówka an accurate picture of their members.

The second part was the distribution of goods. All goods were to be distributed through Dad and he could check the warehouses. This resulted in a big shakeup. It didn't take long for him to discover all the theft going on at the warehouses. The thieves were employees who were falsifying the books. He told his boss and submitted his resignation. He didn't want headaches and preferred to go back to his former job. Muttermilch came to see him and asked Dad not to leave him with all those sharks.

Dad agreed and proceeded to undermine their systematic theft. Each transport of goods of clothes, and groceries that arrived filled two to three railroad cars. The employees asked him to prolong the distribution as much as he could, only giving the petitioners a small portion of what they were asking for and telling them to come back in four or five weeks. But he didn't do that. He started distributing the goods as fast as possible. It took two weeks to empty the warehouses. The employees of the Placówka were miserable, the population was happy, and Muttermilch was in seventh heaven.

When he had been registering all the Polish citizens, he had come upon three families who had been denied registration because their occupation had been recorded as thieves. Dad told Muttermilch that these families had children and an old patriarch and didn't deserve to be treated differently than anyone else.

In addition to the thieves, there was a group of toughs. One day Dad was in bed with the flu and the distribution stopped, with an explanation placed on the door of the Placówka office. Around noon there was knocking at the door. Mom opened it and five of the tough guys pushed her aside and came in. When they entered their room they stopped, looking confused. They started to excuse themselves. They hadn't believed that Dad was really sick; they were sure it was yet another trick of the Placówka employees. They asked why Dad was living in a room with a dirt floor, in such a narrow bed with a straw mattress over corn husks. Later that afternoon one of them returned with a five gallon can of kerosene as a present. He didn't want to accept any money for it and ran away.

Dad only worked with Muttermilch and the Placówka for four and a half months, until 1943, when the Russian government broke off diplomatic relations with the Polish government-in-exile.

Prison

One day Dad came home for lunch and found Mom gone. Shura told him that two NKVD agents had come and arrested her fifteen minutes before, so Dad ran to the NKVD building and found her in the yard with countless other people. They had come looking for him and since he wasn't there, they had taken her instead. He presented himself at the desk and said he was Buszejkin. He was told he had to take Soviet citizenship and return his amnesty papers now that his government had forgotten about him. He said okay, but that his wife would need to be released so she could go home and bring the papers. He told Mom to go hide in the houses of their Kazakh neighbors, and to change the place every day, until the situation was resolved.

Mom didn't return and Dad was arrested and imprisoned together with all his colleagues from the Placówka. There were about 40 people. The arrest chamber had no glass in the windows, just grates; the only good thing was that it had a wooden floor since there were no beds. They spent three weeks there. Not one of the Polish enclave took Soviet citizenship. They all either went to jail or into hiding.

The Soviets tried all kinds of ways to get them to take citizenship: brainwashing, interrogations that went on through the night, threatening them with Siberia, or that they would break up their families. They told Dad that Mom had already taken papers, but he knew that was a lie because he had told her not to, under any circumstances, even deportation.

Here they kept sixty people together like sardines. All the top brass from the Placówka were there with the exception of Muttermilch who had been taken to special quarters. The three families of thieves were there and the second night they took Dad aside. They wanted to murder the six top brass from the Placówka as revenge for the treatment they had received from them. They had razor blades hidden in their clothes that they could use. It took considerable persuasion to convince them not to.

Every day another group of men washed the floor. When his turn came, the thieves wouldn't allow him to do the work and one of them replaced him. But Dad objected. He said he couldn't allow that because his colleagues were doing their turn. So the thieves replaced Dad and the six top brass that they might have murdered. They were professional thieves with a lot of character and a sense of morality.

After three weeks they were taken to a regular jail. The cell in the regular jail was a big room with 26 beds and 207 people. Two barrels served as the "Men's Room." Gregori Magadalan, a railroad thief referred to as the "herszt," or ringleader, was in for the fifth time, this time for three years. He ordered the new guys to sleep by the two barrels. The barrels each had four handles with which to carry and empty them out. With 207 people, many who had dysentery, they filled up quickly and would spill over.

They each received 600 grams of bread a day. Dad divided his in three and ate one every eight hours, but the last one he kept under his head at night. For two consecutive nights, that piece vanished. On the third night he decided he would catch the thief. To his surprise, it was Rubel, the "vice-herszt." He was a big, fat guy, said to be a professional murderer. Four months earlier he had been released and returned four days later after killing a lonely old woman who lived close to the railroad tracks in the northern part of town.

Dad gave him a straight punch, followed with a cross and they started to fight. All the men woke up to watch while one watched at the door. It took all of Dad's fighting skill and all of his desperation to knock the guy out after three minutes. Then came the surprise. Magadalan ordered Rubel to take his things and to lay down on the floor close to a window, and he gave Dad Rubel's bed. The 26 beds were used by the elite who were all murderers and thieves. Magadalan and Rubel had their own, the rest shared two men to a bed.

The next morning Dad had a talk with Magadalan. He told him he was grateful for his elevating him to vice-hersht, but he didn't feel right sleeping in a bed when all his friends were sleeping on the floor near the barrels, and planned to go back with them. With that, Magadalan ordered three beds to be vacated and Dad's friends Czapanski, Iuz Pornas, Judge Dreublott-Rojanski, Zaufal, Kostrezewa, and Dembiniski got beds. For the remaining five weeks in prison, they lived in comfort compared to the beginning of their incarceration. They had beds, and no one stole their bread.

The bandits would play cards, and the winner could take the shoes from a victim that his partners chose. The shoes would be given to the guard who sold them and brought back cigarettes, tobacco, and the Pravda newspaper that was good for rolling paper. From time to time, some of the prisoners would be removed and new ones introduced. Those were mostly Kazakh or Uzbek army deserters.

Interrogations would last most of the night but there were no beatings. Their method was for two agents to sit behind a dish of good food, smoking cigarettes and blowing the smoke in your face, asking if you wanted one, but not giving it to you. They would tell you that all this will be yours if you take citizenship. But no one succumbed. It wasn't heroism, it was simply knowing that if you took citizenship you would be doomed to remain in the Soviet Union for the rest of your life and that was like being in prison, only a much larger one.

At his interrogation, Dad was amazed at how much they knew about his life in Poland and his work for the Placówka. At one point, without thinking, Dad inadvertently gave away a man who had brought 150 horses over the Mongolian border. He said it was the biggest blunder he made in his life. Later, when they let them go, this poor man remained in jail.

While in jail, Mom, dressed as a peasant, would come to visit daily and bring things. The second day, while eating an onion she had brought, he discovered a piece of paper that had been layered in that said "News from the outside. Hold on. Don't take papers. Help will soon arrive from London." That was a morale boost for Dad and for his friends.

One night in early May, 1943, Dad woke up perspiring calling out "Mama, Mama!" Three years later, when they returned to Poland, Adek Lewin told him that his parents were taken to Majdanek in May 1943.

The Russians in jail slept most of the day and told tales at night. These were about their sex lives when they were free men, murders they had done, wheeling and dealing. For Dad these terrible stories were like lullabies that put him to sleep. He could have slept well if it wasn't for the nighttime interrogations.

Dysentery was another problem. People kept dying from it and new interns – mostly deserters -- would take their place. Dad also succumbed.

It was Gregori Magadalan who came to his rescue. Magadalan told him to stop drinking completely and to eat as much *talkan* as he could. Talkan is barley that is toasted, dried, and ground in a mortar. It is rich in nutritional properties and minerals, such as zinc, chromium, selenium, magnesium, B vitamins, fiber, and others. Talkan is produced by all the Turkic peoples of Siberia, Asia and the Caucasus. It is an energy-rich product that regulates digestion, promotes the growth of lactic acid bacteria and thus supports the immune system, and lowers the level of cholesterol in the blood.

It isn't likely that Magadalan knew much of this, but talkan was an indigenous food known to his people and widely eaten. It is often made into a porridge with water, oil, and salt. It can also be used in the preparation of fillings for sausages. Mixing it with water and milk and allowing it to rest for a few days will produce a lightly fermented beverage called bouza. Without water, it was almost impossible to swallow, but Did managed and in three days he was cured. He marveled that you never knew where help would come from in extreme conditions. This time it wasn't a doctor, but the professional railroad thief, Gregori Magadalan, someone Dad never forgot.

There was an old man with two sons who slept on the floor near Dad. They were known in the city as rich, big time operators, buying and selling things and traveling to do their business. The father became sick with dysentery and in a few days the poor old man died. Before they took him away, the two sons started to tear up his pants and gold coins fell out onto the floor. They eagerly took the coins and put them in their pockets. Dad knew what would come next, but could do nothing.

That night Rubel and two other of the bandits approached the young men and ordered them to hand over the coins. Then they started a meticulous search of their clothes and found more coins sewn into their pants and underwear. They took them all. The two young men were crying like babies, which they hadn't done when their father died.

Looking back, Dad thought his experience of the Russian jail where they put over 200 men in a room with only 26 beds, a jail that mixed political prisoners with professional murderers and criminals was unique. He thought the jailers had probably done that on purpose to create an environment that would make conditions so hard that the political prisoners would break down and accept Russian citizenship. He thought the system was unique, but it isn't.

He learned that all kinds of men have their own code of ethics. For example, in his first fight with Rubel, no one tried to help Rubel, even though he was one of the gang and they were in a position of power. No one gave Dad a push or put out a leg for him to trip on and fall. They could have annihilated Dad and his friends easily, and given themselves something to talk about later during the long winter months, but they didn't.

After 40 days, Dad was called one night for interrogation. The NKVD officer said, "For the last time we ask you, will you take Russian citizenship?" "No, because I am a Polish citizen. Your government acknowledged that fact, giving me my amnesty papers in 1942." "Where are these papers?" "I don't know. My wife went to find them." "For living on Soviet territory without proper papers, you are sentenced to two years." "That is not too much. Thank you."

Dad's friends all did the same. They were the first group to refuse. Over one million others did the same, and the Soviet authorities didn't know what to do with them.

Twenty days later Dad was called before the same tribunal. "Would you accept non-citizen papers? You will be a man without a country." "Yes, I accept." Two more days and all of them left the Russian prison. They were free from jail, but not free men. They weren't free until they left the Soviet Union in 1946.

The day after his release, Dad went to see Kosmin who greeted him with two kisses on both cheeks and gave him back his old job. Dad started to work immediately. Their finances and food supplies had gone down to zero, but he was happy to see the barren steppe, the Kazakhs, and everything else after sixty days in jail.

He lost no time in building up their stocks. After five days of bringing home sacks of food and a *czajnik* (kettle) full of sour cream, which usually became butter and skim milk due to riding on the horse, they were back to having a reserve.

The next two years went smoothly. There was the newly formed Polish government-in-exile in Russia headed by Wanda Wasilewska that was probably partly responsible for freeing the Polish citizens from prison. There were organized committees of Polish patriots headed by former Polish communists or fellow travelers. They pressured Dad to work for the new Placówka, but

Dad argued that his work at the kolkhozes was more important for the final goal of breaking the back of the German armed forces. That seemed to convince the patriots, but his name was popular among the Polish people, and the new Placówka wanted to use him for their own propaganda. So he promised to to help part time as a cultural representative.

They expected him to organize lectures with political overtones, but he only gave one lecture on human prejudice throughout history, talking about black cats crossing one's path, and the number thirteen. He engaged in no politics for the next two years. He did organize dances in the local Kazakh high school, and they had an Olympiad of Polish folk dances. Mom taught a group of young people some dances and they won the first prize

With the end of the war in 1945, it was just a matter of time before they would be able to leave "proletariat heaven." Some people who had money, bought their way out early. The organized evacuation began on 12 April 1946. They knew a few weeks in advance when the first convoy would leave and who would be on it.

Lolek and Evacuation

Three weeks before their evacuation, at 2:30 in the morning, a knock on their door woke them up. It was Lolek Pianko and his wife, and they were scared to death. Dad knew Lolek from Warsaw where he had been a rich playboy and a good tennis player. His wife told them their story.

Lolek had been working at a slaughter house and would steal meat by hiding it in his pants, whereupon his wife would sell it to her steady customers. With time, he became an inspector. This allowed him to forget about shoving meat down his pants. Now he could steal a third of a railway car. He didn't work alone. His partners in this business were his boss, the chief bookkeeper, manager of the railroad station, and some military men, with each person receiving a piece of the pie. The police could be bought; it was only a matter of the price.

Everything went smoothly until the NKVD discovered the malversation. You couldn't buy the NKVD. Everyone put the blame on Lolek who escaped from Dzhambul nine months earlier, leaving his wife and two kids at home. He started to hide in different towns and different republics. Finally, he went back home. He didn't know how to hide anymore and had nowhere else to go. So they came to Dad and Mom and asked them to hide Lolek in their house. They figured that Dad and Mom were beyond suspicion, no one would think to look there, so it would be safe. The risk was that if he were found, Mom and Dad could be sent to prison.

The evacuation was supposed to start in three weeks and Mom and Dad felt they couldn't refuse. Dad told him that at night he would sit under or in the apple tree in the back garden, and during the day he would stay under their bed. Mom had customers who came during the day to measure or pick up clothing she made for them. Lolek probably had a good time watching it all from his hiding place.

On the day of their evacuation, Dad wrapped Lolek in blankets, loaded him on a wagon together with the rest of their belongings, and took him to their railroad car (eight horses or forty men). His wife and children went to another car. After that it was easy. On the way back to Poland, no one checked them or their papers. They could have smuggled a dozen Loleks.

Dad always spoke well of the Russian people but he didn't like the government or the NKVD. He told the story of a man and woman who came to their home a few days before the evacuation. The husband was a high officer of the NKVD, dressed in full uniform. Dad and Mom were worried because Mom's work was illegal; no one could work for themselves. But this man's wife was a client and he was friendly and started to talk about their imminent departure. Then, all of a sudden, he took out his communist party membership card and said, "If I could go where you are going, I would tear this thing to pieces." He wasn't drunk. He was typical of the population. If all two hundred million Soviet citizens could leave, there probably wouldn't be a living soul left.

That was Dad's opinion, many years after his wartime Soviet experience. He said that in the history of Russia, they were the first mass group of people who were free to leave. The Russian people they knew didn't believe they were really going home to Poland. They were telling them that it was a trick; that they were going to be sent to Siberia. But they were wrong.

After eighteen days of travel, they stopped at the Soviet/Polish border for a few hours. This was in a forest and Dad took the opportunity to go into the forest to look for flowers. He came back with a bunch of lilies of the valley that were growing wild. It was the 30th of April, my mother's birthday. That was one story I had never heard. I only knew that from as early as I could remember, lily of the valley was her favorite flower and was what we would get her every year for her birthday.

They stopped at Poznan to change trains, but instead of continuing in the same direction, Dad decided to go another way. This was because three months earlier, a couple named Fenigstein had convinced Dad to give them money. Fenigstein was a jeweler who had papers to go through Moscow to Poland. He had been buying and selling gold and diamonds while living in Dzhambul and told Dad he could buy for him also. My parents had saved 1500 rubles during all their six years in the Soviet Union. Dad gave them their money and never heard from them again.

On the train they heard that the couple was in Lodz, so Dad decided to go there and get his money. He found them his first day there, at 11:00

at night. When they saw him, they were scared to death and tried to explain their reasons for not contacting him. Dad asked for the money and they handed it to him. Then he asked if they could sleep on the floor and the couple agreed. The next day they went to Warsaw.

Marysia in Uzbek costume
Kazakhstan c.1944

Post War

Warsaw

The same day that Dad arrived in Warsaw in May 1946, he found a government job at the *Centralny Urząd Planowania* (CVP, Central Planning Office) in the department of agriculture. Their friend, Adek Lewin and his wife Helenka lived in a rented a room with one bed, and they invited Dad and Mom to stay with them where they slept on the floor.

During their six years in the Soviet Union, my parents had no idea what Hitler did to Poland and the Jews. Dad wrote that Adek told him his parents had been taken to Majdanek in May 1943, but he also wrote, in a later section, that Adek told him they were taken in late April 1943 to Treblinka. I don't think he ever knew details of what happened to his parents and the rest of the family. If he did, he never mentioned it and didn't write about it. But after he died, among his possessions I found a photograph of a headstone. It names Abram Buszejkin and Sonia Buszejkin and says they were murdered at Treblinka in May 1943. I assume he had this stone made in 1981 and took the photo that year on his one and only return visit to Warsaw. All the family had remained – Abram, Sonia, Ignacy, Dora, Rena, Estusia, and Kuba – and all had been murdered by the Nazis.

The city was in ruins. Dad found a few friends who had survived, some in Russia, some hidden by neighbors, some who had been partisans in the *Armia Krajowa* or Home Army, a resistance movement in German-occupied Poland, formed in February 1942.

After work Dad would go to Leszno 56, where he and his parents used to live. There were no buildings left standing, only remnants of a house, a wall, an eternal flame, and lots of flowers. It had been the site where the Germans had shot Jews and Poles.

The former Warsaw Ghetto was an uneven field covered with weeds. The only building one could see was the church, standing like a miracle on Nowolipki. Dad would walk through Warsaw where his friends used to live and found only skeletons of houses. He went alone one Sunday to Piaseczno, a residential suburb of Warsaw and found an empty, broken-down place without a living soul. He had the feeling of walking over a huge cemetery without the tombstones. And so his friends were there too with no tombstones.

Three weeks after moving in with Adek and Helenka, Dad made a lucky find of a room in the Praga neighborhood. It was a huge living room with a crystal chandelier and a piano. When he happened to meet his stowaway Lolek Pianko on the street, he helped him to rent a room next door.

After working for four months, Dad was promoted to the post of director of the agriculture department. This meant that he was in control of all the ten agriculture industries in Poland. He received a Jeep with a chauffeur who was armed with a machine gun, and was given a Browning to use. At first everyone at work thought he was Russian because he dressed like one. But he didn't have any other clothes.

When Yom Kippur came, he told the secretary that he would not be coming in to work the next day. When she asked why, he told her "Because it is our biggest holiday, and also it is a holiday for the dead." Thus they learned that he was Jewish.

Czesław Bobrowski, the director of the CVP and the main secretary Maria were both very helpful to Dad. When he first arrived he wrote that he looked like a typical Ivan – that is, he was dressed from head to toe in Russian clothes. Bobrowski and Maria helped him get European clothes. In a short time he underwent a complete transformation with all his new suits, vests, and ties. They also obtained everything necessary for their home.

The first week in Warsaw, he wrote to his aunt Fania, Max's wife, and asked her to help them to emigrate from Europe to anywhere. When he learned that Raya Goldin was also in New York, he wrote to her as well and asked for intervention. And then he wrote to the Szumraks, also asking for help to emigrate.

Raya was very helpful, coordinating the efforts of the two families of relatives. Then one day, he received a letter from the Consul of the Dominican Republic in Paris, telling him that they would have two immigration visas for him and Mom. It was like a miracle.

Then another miracle happened. Through a school friend, he made contact with Helenka Neufeld who was in Paris. Helenka and her husband Henry Mann were waiting for them at the Gare du Nord when they arrived in Paris.

Paris and Nancy

Helenka and Henry took them to a modest hotel in the IX Arrondissement. As refugees they were given coupons for food and a visa to stay in France for thirty days. The atmosphere at the hotel was terrible: dirty and noisy. One of their neighbors was a beautiful prostitute with a flourishing business. She received many phone calls, but the phone was a common phone for the floor, located in the hall. She would step out to answer the phone completely naked but for a silk scarf with which she covered her breasts.

Dad took one day to go by himself to Nancy, the town he had left in a hurry seven years before. He wanted to see who he might find there, what the Place Stanislaw looked like, how his old landlady was. His first visit was to the Association General d'Etudiants where all the faces were new and young. He quickly left. His landlady didn't recognize him. Her old cat, who had died at the end of the First World War, was still lying on her bed, just like before, stuffed with straw and looking out with glass eyes.

Near the railroad station he found his motorcycle mechanic. "Rafał, how are you my old man?" he asked, before Dad could even say a word. They spent an hour talking and then, with his spirit lifted, he boarded the train back to Paris.

Nice

Dad decided they would leave Paris and wait for their visas on the French Riviera. In September 1946, they went to Nice in the Department of Alps Maritime, one of two departments that was closed to refugees, and found a modest room near the Promenade des Anglais at Boulevard Francois Grosso 6. All my life, I had heard about their time living at this small pension near the Promenade des Anglais. It was only when I was in my late 40s that my mother told me it was actually a disreputable hotel and she had been the only non-working girl there. They stayed there for seven months.

Dad set off immediately to find Solomon Pelix, the cousin who, years before, had given up riches to return to his longshoreman work and his prostitutes in Marseille. Solomon was now happily married to Nanette with whom he had a son who was one and a half years old. He owned a small factory that made bitter orange marmalade for the local stores and hotels and invited Dad to come and work with him. Dad worked four hours a day at the factory and the rest of the day he delivered jellies to the local stores and hotels, pedaling a tricycle with a box at the back.

Dad spent weekends at the beach mixing with the well-off tourists and playboys who were spending their winter on the Riviera. On Sundays he would rent a yellow Peugeot with red leather seats and take Mom driving up and down the coast. They visited the Oceanographic Museum in Monaco, and were careful not to play roulette. Their seven months in Nice were probably some of the happiest of their lives; they were young, good-looking, and happy to be free.

My mother was seven months pregnant with me when they left on 20 April 1947 and flew from Orly to La Guardia in New York. Her gynecologist in Nice had advised her to drink a lot of beer.

New York

When they arrived at La Guardia, the immigration officer asked how long they wanted to stay in the U.S., and Dad made the mistake of timidly asking if they could stay for two weeks. He didn't know that if he had asked for a longer stay, they might have given them two or three months and I might have been born in New York, allowing them to automatically become U.S. citizens. But no one had told him of that possibility beforehand, and he was worried about only being allowed to stay for two or three days.

Dad found those two weeks unpleasant. There seemed no end to the parties to meet relatives, and they were tired, especially Mom, being seven months pregnant. Everyone came with cameras to take pictures. No one seemed to know much about the Holocaust. Some were more friendly and understanding: Rafał and Aunt Besia, Aunt Fania, Włodek Alapin, and Raya, but even they didn't tell him that they could prolong their stay because of Mom's advanced stage of pregnancy. Dad never knew whether that was because of negligence, lack of information, or if they were afraid if they stayed they would become a burden.

Dad went to the Jewish Agricultural Society where, by chance, he met David Stern. Stern was also an agronomist and had graduated from Nancy six years before Dad. He was (or had been) the unofficial head agronomist in Palestine. He told Dad that in the Dominican Republic there was a colony of refugees, mostly from Austria and Germany. It was a farm cooperative that produced milk. It had been organized in 1936 by American philanthropists, who contributed two and a half million dollars, and the Dominican government under President Rafael Leónidas Trujillo, who wanted as many white people as possible to come to the island. Sosua had six hundred founding members, some Christians, mostly Jewish, some mixed marriages, and some unmarried men.

There had been three unsuccessful directors until the American investors finally hired David Stern, bringing him from Palestine. He got the milk and the milk by-products production running and got the insubordinate German Jews in line. He told Dad to wait for him in a small pension in the capital that was managed by a woman who was one of the early German refugees. Stern went to Palestine to get his family and Dad and Mom went to Ciudad Trujillo to wait.

Sosua, Dominican Republic

The tropical heat was terrible. They had already experienced mosquitoes in Siberia, but for Mom it was far more difficult now because she was seven months pregnant.

When Stern arrived, it was with his two sons and a daughter. His wife had been killed by a bomb that had been thrown in a public bus. They all went to Sosua.

Spanish-speaking Dominican Republic is situated on the eastern side of the island Hispaniola; French-speaking Haiti is located on the western part. Sosua is located on the northern shore of the Dominican half of the island. At that time, both were governed by dictators: Trujillo and Papa Duvalier. The Dominican Republic was 85% black and 15% white, descendants of the Spanish conquistadors. The population was 15% rich, people living comfortable lives, and 85% poor, people who were living day-to-day. There was essentially no middle class.

They arrived at Puerto Plata on the Atlantic, and then drove 27 bumpy kilometers to Sosua, where each settler had 100 acres of land for pasturing cows, each one fenced with barbed wire. A settler received a ready-made farm consisting of the 100 acres, a two-room house furnished with caoba (mahogany) furniture, two horses, ten rams for the head of the family, two cows for the mother, and one cow for each child, as well as some chickens and pigs. All this cost $9,000 and was to be paid in 99 years. In addition to their farm, everyone had a job at the cooperative, school, or administration.

A few weeks after their arrival in Sosua, Mom gave birth to me. At the time, they were still staying at Sonia's hotel on the seashore and one quarter of a mile away was the "hospital." The doctor had been milking cows for the last six years. When the old doctor immigrated to the US, the young one started his practice on Mom and me.

Labor started on June 18 at about 3:00 p.m. and they went to the hospital immediately with Dad spending the night in the waiting room. At 8:00 the next morning, the young doctor came out and said "Go take a nap in the hotel. I don't expect anything to happen before the evening." Dad headed back to the hotel, but walking along the beach, the water looked so inviting and refreshing and the beach was empty, so he decided to take a swim.

He was out past the breakers, swimming to shore, when all of a sudden he saw a white horse with a rider who was waving his arms. He looked around, but there was no one in the water but him. He swam back to shore and the man handed him a letter written in Russian. "Congratulations with a daughter," signed Stern.

Dad took the horse from the messenger and was at the hospital in two minutes. There, he found the doctor waiting for him with the placenta. "Everything went okay, the only thing is here," and he showed Dad the placenta. "I think," he continued, "there is some piece missing. I was afraid of complicating the matter. I wanted to suggest that you take your wife to the hospital in Puerto Plata. Do I have your okay?"

Dad examined the placenta, which he said was quite similar to that of a cow. On both sides were impressions of the hip bones. He told this to the doctor who quieted down some and then he told him that if they took Mom to Puerto Plata, which was 27 kilometers on a small, bumpy road, they could expect real complications. The doctor agreed.

Then Dad got his first look at me: "a small red thing with a few dark blond hairs." "She looks like me," he said to the nurse. "Yes, that's your copy," she answered. Apparently he didn't really feel like a father until eight months later when he put me in front of him on the saddle and we galloped along the beach in the sand.

Dad's first duties were to familiarize himself with the general condition of the farming, to help build new settlements, and to clear some of the existing tropical jungle. At the site of the new development, called Choko, he met the foreman, Hans Lesser, a very warm man who was almost eaten up by the mosquitoes. He was Evangelical German, his wife was a Polish Jew.

The water they were drinking had a terrible stench. It was taken from a cement reservoir built to conserve water, but no one had considered the algae that was growing on the cement. Dad advised Hans to remove all the water, clean the reservoir, then melt paraffin and apply it to the walls and the floor. They soon had fresh water to drink.

Dad was responsible for the installation of vegetable gardens in all of the 150 farms. By that time, he had already set up his own and Mom sold the vegetables, riding her mare with sacks attached to the back of her saddle. They made three times as much from the sale of the vegetables than the sale of milk to the cooperative from his thirteen cows.

He had a hard time installing the gardens. The men were never at their farms. Instead they were at the cafes or the two bowling alleys. Each of them had a peon so most of the time he worked with the helpers, otherwise the project not only would not have finished, it never would have even started. Finally all the gardens were done and flourishing, but no one bothered to maintain the gardens, preferring to buy from Dad, so Mom kept up her deliveries.

Dad also seeded a small field of corn, and it grew so well that a newspaper from the capital sent a photographer and put a photo of the corn on their front page. It wasn't easy preparing the field. Dad worked for weeks with his peon, Antonio Almonte, breaking up the coral rocks to even the surface and then haul top soil in with wheelbarrows. He promised Antonio that he would receive a bonus of ten percent of the total corn. He received twelve one-hundred kilogram sacks. The rest of the farmers were angry, saying that Dad was spoiling "the natives." But Dad said that Antonio worked just as hard as he did and he fully deserved his pay.

Antonio was a giant of a man, not tall but built like an Apollo and very dark. He was completely loyal to both of them. He would babysit me once a week when Mom and Dad went to the cinema. Even if they returned late, he would insist on taking off the saddles and taking the horses to pasture. Sometimes they would get back at 1:30 a.m. and milking started at 4:30. Dad started to teach him boxing. He was a promising boxer and when Dad left the Dominican Republic he promised to send him papers to immigrate to the U.S., but Antonio never got permission to leave.

They had a maid called Dorilla. She had been living with a partner for over four years until he immigrated to the U.S., leaving her alone. She never got over it. She was a good worker and good with me. One month, after receiving her pay, she spent it all on a bottle of perfume which she used up the same evening. Her chores ended at 9:30 p.m. Then she would wash, dress, and disappear only to reappear again to milk the cows and take the milk from Ramona, the best cow, for me. Once in a while she would disappear for two or three weeks. When she came back she would explain that it was necessary for her to live in her native manner, it was "like a breath of fresh air," she would say. As for her nightly escapades, she would say "I have to have a man every night. Our blood, señora, is not like yours, half mixed with water."

One day two Americans came to our home. They had heard that there was a Polish couple with a small girl living in the jungle and they had come to take a look. Dad wasn't home and they told Mom they would come back the following weekend.

They were Alfred Shenker and Mr. Jurikowski, both originally from Poland. They were both millionaires and were building a chocolate factory in Puerto Plata. When they came back, they took Dad 270 kilometers to see the American Consul who examined all of his papers and told him that in about six weeks he would be able to enter the U.S. on a preference quota because he was an agronomist. This was a huge event for them, especially for Mom who disliked Sosua.

Jurikowski and Shenker had met in New York at the 1939 World Fair when they were both penniless. Shenker, a chemist by profession, had owned a big chocolate-waffles factory in Kracòw before the war. Jurikowski had an import/export business in Warsaw and was also quite a rich man. Once they met in New York, they decided to join forces. Shenker produced the chocolate waffles and Jurikowski sold them. Jurikowski made some smart business moves, and Shenker used to call him "A goy with a Jewish head."

About three months after the Puerto Plata factory went into production trouble started. President Trujillo owned 49% of the factory. His government instigated a march on the factory, demanding the factory be Dominican, not American. Shenker and Jurikowski were forced to turn over shares, leaving them with 49% and Trujillo with 51%. A month later he did it again, setting up demonstrations in Puerto Plata. This time it was to demand nationalization of the factory. So he paid off the two partners and took possession.

Syphilis

One day Mom felt a terrible pain in her abdomen. Dad put her on a bus to Puerto Plata and came home to stay with me. It was appendicitis. The operation was successful and she was back home in eight days.

But soon after her operation, the nightmare started. At a checkup to see that the incision was healing properly, Mom was told she had syphilis and that she would have to go for penicillin shots twice a week. After three weeks, the doctor said she was cured, but he wanted to do a blood test on Dad. To his surprise, it was positive. This meant that Dad had to take the bus to Puerto Plata twice a week for injections.

In the meantime, the six weeks promised by the American Consul was approaching. They were staying at that same pension in the capital and had no income. When they arrived there, the woman who ran the place told Dad that she had heard about his bad luck from the doctor in Puerto Plata who would give him a few more injections and he would be okay. This was when it occurred to him that maybe the whole thing was a hoax. But he put the idea out of his mind. The injections were costing $25 a week so Dad wrote to family in New York to ask for help until their visas came.

After the six weeks had passed and there was no news from the American Consul, Dad decided to look for a job in the capital. One morning he found in the local newspaper that someone was looking for a gardener. He was going to go in his work clothes, but Mom insisted he dress in the best he had. He didn't agree, but did as she suggested, and walked the 40 minutes to the address given in the paper. With the hotel, living expenses, and the injections to pay for, he was desperate to find a job.

He had expected to find a vegetable/kitchen garden. Instead he found himself standing before a handmade gate leading to a park and a mansion. He rang the bell and a butler opened the door. He told him he wanted to apply for the gardener's position and was told that Dr. Parra would be with him in a few minutes.

Dr. Parra was an immaculately-dressed white man. He introduced himself as Frank Parra, Minister of Finances of the Dominican Republic. Dad asked him to forgive his intrusion, but he thought they needed a gardener. He wanted Dad to tell him about himself. It took half an hour for him to tell Parra his story. Parra listened attentively and seemed impressed.

Finally he said, in good French, "Yes, you are in the proper place and I can use a man like you." He had some tree work that needed to be done. Dad wouldn't work physically, he would supervise the two gardeners. He asked how much Dad wanted a month. Dad told him $80, which would be enough to cover his expenses. Parra told him he would pay $125. He would start the next day and a chauffeur would come to pick him up and take him home as it was too hot to walk in the humid heat.

Dad was amazed. When he came home to tell Mom the good news, she said "Was I right about the clothes?" Yes, she was. The next morning the black limousine was there at 8:15 in front of their modest hotel.

After working on the mansion grounds for three days, Parra came and asked him if he had left a job application at the fruit juice and soda factory in town. Dad had, two weeks before. It turned out that Parra was the president of the company and Trujillo was the owner and they had a mess. The technical director was Jose Santos Rodriguez, an entomologist and refugee from Franco's Spain. Parra said "He probably knows a lot about bugs but little about factory machinery and production." He wanted Dad to go there after lunch to see if he could help out.

Dad met Santos Rodriguez with whom he became friends. The state of affairs at Exploitation des Fruitos Dominicanos was terrible. One of Trujillo's cousins was in charge of buying all the necessary machinery for production from the U.S. Before starting to work at the factory, this man had been a cosmetics salesman, and he didn't know what he was doing. He bought new machinery, making a nice commission for himself on the side, but no one knew how to organize the equipment into a chain of production. Having had some experience with the bitter oranges in Nice, Dad prepared new recipes for the oranges. Even the pigs had refused to eat the other. The oranges were abundant as was the sugar, and the labor was cheap. They could outprice anyone.

After a few days, Dad started to spend all his time working at the factory where he worked for another half year, waiting for their American visas and taking the weekly syphilis injection. It seemed like the visas would never come and the illness would never go away. But finally one day, a call came from the Consul that their visas were ready to be picked up at any time.

Before going to the consulate, Dad stopped at the doctor to tell him he was about to leave. "Don't you worry," he said. "We will give you an extra special injection which will cure you instantly with no reoccurrence and then I will give you your certificate of health. This shot will cost you $150." By then, Dad had finally figured out that he was the victim of a scam, but there was nothing he could do. He needed the certificate. In any case, the golden-egg-laying goose was flying the coop.

Later, in New York, Dad met a butcher from Sosua who told him his syphilis story. The butcher told him that almost everyone they knew had the same experience but were afraid to speak up. It was the only way to leave the country. He and his wife had also had injections for three months and then, finally, one miracle injection that cured both of them instantly. "They know you have rich relatives in the States, and that makes you a good milking cow."

Parra offered to pay him $350 a month, instead of $125 if he would stay another year with them. But Dad boarded a plane the next day by himself and went to New York to prepare a place for Mom and me to come to, not asking for any help from relatives.

c. 1946

On the French Riviera, 1946

Sosua, c. 1948

Sosua

Corn, Sosua

A New World

New York

He arrived in New York on 7 June 1949, and three days later, through the Jewish Agricultural Society, he had a job in New Jersey as a farm hand on a chicken farm. The job came with a huge furnished house for us. Mom and I joined him on the 23rd, just a few days after my second birthday.

One day the owner asked Dad to paint the old chicken coops with some solution. He finished the job at lunchtime and soon after the trouble started. He had burned his hands with the creosote. No one had warned him of the danger and no one had supplied rubber gloves. The owner, Mr. Peck, took him to a doctor. He was not able to work for two weeks. Mom didn't like the life on the farm, so we moved to New York where the Joint provided us with a small room with a kitchenette on 87th and Broadway at Capitol Hall.

While staying at Capitol Hall, we met the Stachel family. Luba was Russian, and Felix was Polish and had fought with the partisans during the war. I don't know where they met, but they had their daughter, Telsa, in a displaced persons camp in Germany in 1946. The two couples hit it off and remained good friends for the rest of their lives.

Raya's brother offered Dad a job at the factory that he was managing where they dried vegetables, packed them, and sold them to stores.

Dad had the night shift with a black fellow by the name of Joe. They worked together putting the vegetables that had been prepared during the day into the electric ovens to dry. Dad was making 90 cents an hour.

While many of the Jewish refugees had trouble finding any job at all, Dad was always looking for something better and had many jobs during the five years that we lived in New York. After the dried vegetables, he found a job on the corner of Broadway and Eighth in downtown Manhattan where the factory was in the cellar, and he worked fixing tools for the girls. There were over thirty of them, Spanish-speaking from Puerto Rico. He made suggestions for improvements and Mr. Blum listened, put them into practice, and was very pleased with the results. After two months, he made Dad the foreman. He was generous, gave Dad bonuses, and when he had the flu, he sent an extra check for $150.

One Sunday they went to visit Mr. Shenker at his estate in New Jersey. Dad had bought himself a panel truck for $145 and every day a part of the body would fall off. He parked this truck among the Cadillacs, Mercedes, and Continentals. He felt miserable in the parking lot, but at the reception it was different. They were the center of attention – heroes saved by Shenker and Jurikowski from the tropical jungle.

Shenker offered Dad a job at his factory in the Bronx. So Dad said goodbye to Mr. Blum and the girls, thanking him for everything. We changed our accommodation, renting a room and a kitchen from a family, and he started to travel from Brooklyn to the Bronx, an hour and twenty minutes each way. He worked mostly loading sugar and molasses into big vats of boiling water.

After three weeks, Shenker's younger brother promoted him to assistant chief mechanic. His duties started at 5:00 a.m. when he would heat up twenty-four big gas ovens, check to see that they functioned, and fix them if something was wrong. At 7:00 a.m. his boss, the chief mechanic, would come and ask if everything was okay, take a cup of coffee from a dispenser, and start reading the newspaper. Everything went along nicely for six months and then his venture in horticulture began.

One evening, Hans Lesser from Sosua came to visit with his new wife. He told Dad they lived in Queens and he was working outdoors for a landscape gardener and making $1.25 an hour. Dad was making $1.10 working indoors.

Until then, Dad hadn't realized there was a possibility of that kind of job in the city. The next day he took the Yellow Pages, looked under gardeners, and found the Polish name Zielinski, Garden Maintenance. He called. The man spoke Polish poorly and told him to come to see him the same afternoon. He worked for Zielinski for three months and learned a lot.

There were six of them working with the boss who was almost always drunk, sleeping in the cab of the truck. His older brother, Joe, managed the work. Joe was a knowledgeable man and a good gardener. He was Dad's best source of information about the job, its secrets and its shortcuts.

When Dad felt he had nothing more to learn there, he found himself a job in New Jersey with a German landscaper who was stronger than a bull and worked like one, but for only seven hours a day, saying "Seven hours is enough for us. I'll pay you for eight at $1.50 an hour." Dad was his only helper. The man knew his work well and once again Dad learned a lot.

Dad noticed an ad in the New York Times for two gardeners at a hospital for chronic diseases. He took a day off from Hans and went to the sanitarium. "Four acres of grounds," said the superintendent. "Those two guys that I dismissed were no good, they couldn't do the job." Dad proposed that he could do the job alone and asked for one and a half the monthly pay which was accepted. He worked five and a half days a week, eight hours a day.

In the meantime, he enrolled in landscape architecture courses by correspondence and finished them in seven months instead of the planned two and a half years. He started to look for additional jobs for the one and a half days he was off and began doing maintenance jobs and planting. Once he had to create wells around three trees in New Jersey after the level of the plot was raised artificially by six feet, and then fill it in with rocks, gravel, and preserve the trunks with charcoal and paper. He did the job in ten hours and made his first big money -- $270 in one day. He decided that getting into landscaping, which was related to his profession, was the right way to go and could be quite lucrative.

One evening he got a call from someone who had picked him out of the telephone directory and who was looking for a job. He turned out to be six feet two and just skin and bones. He was Swiss and had come to live with his father who was a baker and who he hardly remembered because the father had left his mother and never returned. When the mother died, he wrote to his son to come.

Claude had finished gardening school in Switzerland and was 25 years old. He started the next day at the sanitarium. Dad changed his arrangement to working three days a week with his helper for the same pay. For the first time, Dad found someone who worked harder than he did. One day Dad injured his eye while trimming a tree. Dr. Hyaman was the eye doctor who treated him. Later he would employ him. With all his work, the money was rolling in.

Winter was hard, not because there was no money at home, but because Dad couldn't stand sitting around being idle. So he found work trimming large oak trees at the Military Cemetery in Long Island for a few weeks, working with a night cleaning crew at McGraw Hill Publishing in Manhattan for six weeks, and working as a security guard at a chemical factory in Brooklyn.

When spring came, Dr. Hyaman called to say he wanted Dad to come with him to see his summer house in Spring Valley, New Jersey, 75 miles from New York. There were two and a half acres and he wanted Dad to do some landscaping. It was his first big job – over $3000 gross. Dad did the job by hand, not renting any heavy equipment. His crew consisted of six men: one Swiss, one Polish, one Ukrainian, two Puerto Ricans, and one American. They were all good, professional men. The Polish guy was seventy-two and raked perfectly even on the hottest days. Every now and then he would take a flask of vodka and tell them "It's cold. I have to take a swallow or two to warm up."

Once, on a job in Glen Cove, Long Island, Dad contracted with an Italian farmer in Hewlett for twelve five-ton truckloads of topsoil. When the farmer brought the last load, he invited Dad and the crew to come to his home for a glass of wine after work. They stopped off that evening and the farmer's wife gave each of them a very tall glass of red wine which they drank on empty stomachs.

Heading for home in Dad's truck, there were two guys with him in the cab, and four in the back. All of a sudden Dad noticed that they were all singing, Dad included, but each one a different song in a different language. He dropped each one off and was finally left with Claude with whom he sang "Frère Jacques." Half drunk, he got home still singing "Frère Jacques."

Dad said that at first, I was miserable in New York. I couldn't speak English so the other children didn't want to play with me. But in a few weeks that changed. I started going to kindergarten and to dance lessons. I performed a tap dance to The Good Ship Lollipop in a white and bright pink satin costume, holding a big lollipop in each hand. I have a photo of myself in that costume, lest I forget.

My parents were concerned that I learn English so they would speak to me in Polish, but I would speak to them in English. This continued until I was sixteen and my boyfriend started coming to the house. It's a shame that we didn't cultivate both languages so that I could be truly bilingual, because after all those years, I could understand, but could only say what I could say as a two-year-old, when speaking Spanish wasn't a priority and Polish was the language at home: "*Ja potrzebuję siusiu,*" I need to pee, and "*Ja nie chcę,*" I don't want it.

Dad says I was a happy girl with dark blonde hair which became darker each year until it was finally dark brown. Once we went to Coney Island and I recorded two songs: "*Pije Kuba do Jakuba,*" a Polish drinking song that my parents would sing with their friends, and "Goodnight Irene." I vaguely remember those two red disks, and can still sing a few words of that Polish drinking song which I did, not long ago, to the great amusement of an older Polish couple I happened to meet that was vacationing nearby.

My parents' social life was very limited. Dad couldn't forgive his relatives for their having to go unnecessarily to the Dominican Republic. He severed relations with them, with the exception of the two aunts: Besia and Fania.

Besia was 73 and her second husband, Sam, an artist, was 82. They and all their friends lived in Greenwich Village. They introduced their friends, who were all about half her age, to Mom and Dad.

Dad worked for Sam for a few weekends, making molded gypsum copies of African masks, from the originals, for museums to sell to the public. Sam paid Dad $3.50 an hour. At his regular jobs he was making $1.10 to $1.25.

This second marriage didn't last long. Sam was jealous of the elevator man and they divorced in 1950. She kept coming to visit us in Brooklyn, always bringing presents. She was a typical, sweet, old, Bohemian lady.

At Aunt Fania's house, supper was always the same. It must have included chicken soup because whenever I smell it, I think of her home. Her husband, Max, who was also her uncle, was 20 years older. They had two children who died before reaching the age of one. Every day was the same for her, like the day before and the next day. They were rich, retired, living in the midst of huge apartment buildings in Brooklyn. They were the ones who had sent the wool to Siberia. Uncle Max died in 1949. When she died, many years later, she left me a couple of pieces of lovely, old jewelry.

They had a few, but not many friends of their own. Dad met his old school mate Gregory Frydman and his wife Gusta. He was an accountant and helped Dad prepare his tax returns. Although he considered her a good friend, he seldom saw Raya. Luba and Felix Stachel from the Capitol had left for California. Mom and I went to the Catskills for vacations and made some new acquaintances there. But basically, after three years in New York, he had had enough and started to think about California where the climate was better and he could work all year around. All his friends told him it was foolish to go to a new place when he was making a good living where he was. But for Dad, money wasn't everything and a new challenge caught his imagination.

Finally, in the summer of 1954, Mom and I were on vacation in the Catskills, typical of families in those days where the wife and kids would spend time in the mountains while the fathers stayed in the city working and would come up for weekends. Dad built four big boxes, loaded all our belongings, and he was ready to go. When Mom got back to the city, she would have to face the fact. He left us with blankets and pillows he had borrowed from Aunt Fania, and he headed west to California.

He had a new ¾-ton turquoise blue Dodge stake truck, and his load was two and a half tons. He remembers the stretch on the Pennsylvania

Turnpike because (1) you pay for every mile you travel, (2) his right front tire blew out, and (3) he was stopped by the highway patrol. "Where are you going?" "To California." "All by yourself?" "My wife and daughter are waiting for me in Brooklyn. I'll leave my truck in California and return to drive my family by car." "You have a heavy load for such a small truck. Could we take a look inside?" "Sure, you are the policeman."

They uncovered the edge of the canvas that covered the four boxes and some loose landscape equipment. "What is inside those boxes?" "All that we possess." "You built those boxes yourself?" "Yes." "Okay, go to California and good luck to you." Dad considered he was already lucky since they hadn't given him a ticket for overloading.

Dad made a few stops to enjoy seeing the country for the first time. Virginia in the early fall was beautiful, and so were the Ozarks. The Texas prairie had no end. In Arizona there was the painted desert, the meteor, and the Grand Canyon. At the Arizona-California border there was a coyote looking at the truck and howling, then, slowly, he crossed the road and disappeared into the darkness. Each evening when he stopped for the night, he would call home person-to-person, asking for himself, thus letting Mom know where he was and that he was okay.

At his last stop he called Bruce (Boris) Fisher. Bruce was an old school friend from Warsaw who had dropped out before his last year of high school and left Warsaw for the United States in

1938. Dad happened to meet a famous Polish-Jewish actor in New York who gave him Bruce's address in Mar Vista, California. Dad wrote to him, received an answer, and a year later wrote again to say he was coming out.

Los Angeles

From the California border, Dad drove directly to Bruce's house on Woodbine Street where he arrived at four in the morning and parked in front of the house. There were no lights on so he sat in the cab, put his head and arms over the steering wheel, and fell asleep. When he woke up at five-thirty the house was still dark, but at six there were lights at two of the windows so he rang the bell. A man with dense grey hair who resembled Boris opened the door and his arms: "You finally made it!"

Bruce's parents had been theatre actors, and his sister was an actress in Lodz's Municipal Theatre. Bruce was a good sportsman, swimmer, and water polo player. He also liked girls. His last girlfriend with whom he had lived in Warsaw was a medium whose father was Shiller-Shkolnik, a famous clairvoyant. When Bruce was in school he had two dreams: to be a blood brother to a Native American, and to build airplanes.

Bruce now had a wife, three daughters, and a son. He was an engineer and had been working at Hughes Aircraft for the last eight years. He was also a blood brother to the Cherokee Nation and went every year to their big powwow in Arizona. The whole family had all the Native American dress and regalia – at least some of which Bruce had made himself.

Bruce pulled out his car, and Dad parked his truck with all our worldly possessions in the garage, where it would stay for two weeks. He had taken the day off from work so they could spend it together, starting off with breakfast out. Later in the day Dad met the family and finally in the evening Bruce took Dad to the airport for a flight back to New York. Dad fell asleep as soon as he strapped on the seatbelt and remained asleep until the stewardess woke him at La Guardia.

We went to Aunt Fania's for a short visit to return the blankets and pillows and to say goodbye. Then Dad went to buy a new car, an olive green Dodge four-door, three-speed stick shift with the ram's head hood ornament. We left to drive cross-country the next day.

This time it was a tourist drive. It had taken Dad five and a half days driving alone to get to California. This time, stopping along the way, it took nine and a half. First off we drove to the Atlantic shore and Dad stuck his fingers in the water. When we arrived at Santa Monica Beach, at the end of Route 66, he did the same. They had a few thousand dollars saved and for the first three weeks we drove around northern and southern California, enjoying the diversity in the landscape. There were huge mountains, deserts, ocean. It was unbelievable. In southern California the only thing missing was a navigable river.

One beautiful morning Dad pulled out the map to make a plan for our next escapade when Mom pointed out that they had only $150 left. So instead of going on another trip, Dad went to look for work. He found an ad in the newspaper and went to 37th Street and Western Avenue, and a Mexican boss showed him around the retail nursery. He was half drunk and asked when Dad could start. Immediately. Thus began his first day of work on the West Coast.

The pay was low and the work, selling plants and garden supplies, was easy. His boss was always drinking tequila which is why he needed a helper. It would not have been enough work for two sober men. The fourth day the boss drank more than usual and started to swear at Dad in Spanish, not realizing that Dad spoke Spanish. Dad told him back, in Spanish, then changed to Russian, the only language, he said, that you could feel the juice of it when you were swearing. The guy was confused and didn't know what to say. Dad asked for his pay and left.

He bought a paper on his way home, but there were no ads for gardeners or landscapers. Driving along he passed a huge employment office so he stopped and went in to inquire if they had anything for him. Yes, they did, but it was in West Covina. How much did he have to pay if he took the job? Nothing, the employer pays the fee.

So he went to A.A. Schnierow Nursery Systems. This was a huge hot house wholesale enterprise. "Old Man" Schnierow was a Russian Jew who had come to Los Angeles fifty-seven years before and organized the first nursery system for indoor plants. He was quite rich, married to the same woman for forty years, with three married daughters. The three sons-in-law all worked at the nurseries. One of the sons drove a five-ton truck delivering plants all over Southern California and as far north as San Francisco; one worked at the Venice branch; and the third, Louis, was the general accountant of the business.

There were three nurseries in different locations of Los Angeles and Dad was sent to the largest where, besides himself, there was Ed, the foreman, four other men, and two women. The women worked in the propagation section; the men did the rest. Indoor plants were new to Dad so he had to learn the names of the plants in a hurry. The work wasn't easy, but it was a lot less strenuous than landscaping. As a new recruit, they gave him the hardest jobs, but they weren't really hard for him.

One example was when Ed told him to prepare a six foot by six foot hole for a new generator to be installed and gave him eight hours to do it. Dad finished it before lunch and was sitting, resting when AA, the owner, came by. When he learned that Ed had given Dad eight hours for a job he had done in three, he laughed.

"Here is the best example of why Israel grew so fast." He was a Zionist.

Dad worked at the nursery five and a half days a week. After a few weeks, he put an ad in the paper, looking for maintenance and small landscaping jobs. When he started to get some response, he told Ed what he was doing and asked if he could work five days a week. Once he had more than two days of his own work and needed a third day, he quit the nursery.

From then on his business grew quickly. He worked alone, doing landscaping, tree surgery, tree removal, and maintenance.

We rented a house on Hillhurst Avenue in the Los Feliz neighborhood near Griffith Park and a few years later my parents bought a house nearby on Melbourne Avenue. That was a beautiful, two-storey craftsman house with dark wood paneling downstairs, a sleeping porch off the big bedroom, a big back garden, and a gravel driveway shared with the neighbor that led to the side-by-side garages.

One of his early jobs was a small, two-day landscape remodeling in West Hollywood that had been designed by Garrett Eckbo, a well-known landscape architect. Eckbo came to the job when Dad was finishing, was pleased with the work, and asked if he could hire a crew and do more work. Dad said yes so Eckbo gave him his card. That small job changed everything.

He went to the office of Eckbo, Dean, and Williams in Pasadena and they started to give him work. First he hired four men to help, then, during the first three years he had six. For one job he needed 23.

They were both breaking the law because Dad didn't yet have his contractor's license and nevertheless, Eckbo was giving him work. Eckbo also introduced him to Kenneth Reiner, an electrical engineer and a millionaire.

In the early 30s, Reiner came to Los Angeles from New York where he had been living with his parents. His father was an owner of a small chocolate factory. Reiner had recently graduated and was sure he could find employment in the aircraft industry, but he had no luck and returned to New York.

His father suggested he take some chocolate samples and try to take orders on the West Coast. So Reiner came to Los Angeles again, but he had no luck with the chocolates. Not wanting to return home a second time, he again looked for employment in the aircraft industry, and this time he found a job in one of the huge factories that employed hundreds of people. After a few months he married a girl he met on the assembly line.

The second year at the factory, he designed and patented a special lightweight, self-locking aircraft nut. Other patents led to the spring-loaded Lady Ellen Klippies, a ladies hair clip, and he became a rich man.

When Dad met Reiner he was living in the former governor's mansion in Silver Lake, then a poor section of Los Angeles. The mansion had eight acres of land and Dad started to remodel the grounds according to Eckbo's design.

It took Dad five months to complete the work at Bella Vista. Eckbo then told him he wanted him to work on the next Reiner project. This was Silvertop, Reiner's dream house that would incorporate some of his inventions. He bought up around thirty properties on one hill facing Silver Lake, engaged John Lautner to design the house, and Garrett Eckbo to design the landscaping. Dad was the landscape contractor.

John Lautner had worked as an apprentice to Frank Lloyd Wright at Taliesin for six years and continued a working relationship with Wright for years afterwards. He believed in organic architecture, where the houses were integrated into their locations and created an organic indoor-outdoor flow between spaces. Like Wright, many of his houses were sited in elevated locations or difficult sites on hillsides or seashores, taking advantage of the views the sites offered. He also tended to build on the slope, rather than on the top of a hill, and he made use of the latest building materials and technologies, especially in the use of beams and concrete.

Silvertop was a midcentury architectural masterpiece. From its hilltop site in the Silver Lake neighborhood, it enjoyed a many-sided view of Los Angeles. According to Lautner and Reiner, "the house was to be quiet, both to the ear and the eye, and achieve a sense of natural beauty by blending into the natural surroundings." The walls were curved, the kitchen curved into the dining area and the whole space was enveloped by a wall of glass. The cantilevered swimming pool was one of the world's first infinity pools. But it was the sweeping, cantilevered, concrete driveway, only four inches thick and with no supporting columns, that drew the concerned attention of the city building inspectors. Eventually they conducted tests and three firetrucks proved that the driveway could indeed bear the required weight. While Dad and his crew worked on the landscaping, Reiner had a helicopter fly over the site taking photos. Sadly, because of financial problems, Reiner never lived in his dream house.

But he did go on to do other projects and Dad was employed again. This time it was at the Midtown School, designed again by John Lautner. Reiner was not happy with the schooling available for his children, so he decided to create a private school for progressive families – an ethnically balanced school that would include all nationalities living in Los Angeles, and all financial levels. Reiner would subsidize the tuition of those students whose families could not afford to pay. It consisted of a cluster of small hexagonal classrooms and administrative buildings and was located on a six and a half-acre campus on Russell Avenue in the Los Feliz neighborhood.

Reiner invited Dad to enroll me, but he declined, feeling the school was too much ahead of the times. He was especially concerned about the fact that students would not be given grades and classes would not be given according to the age of the students. Later, when he wrote his memoir, he said he was sorry he had declined the offer. On the day of the opening, evidence of Reiner's vision could be seen in the parking lot where fifteen-year-old Chevrolets were parked next to last year's Bentleys.

It was while he was working at the Midtown School that he came home one evening and Mom told him that two men had been asking for him. They left a message that said he had six weeks to produce a state C-27 landscape contractor's license or he would be given a $500-fine and six months in jail. He had been breaking the law by having an ad in the Yellow Pages under Landscape Construction. He still had two months' work to finish the school. They were working from 6:00 a.m. until 1:00 or 2:00 a.m. by electric light. This couldn't have happened to him at a worse time, but he started to study for the exam. He passed both parts, he received his contractor's license, and he was spared the experience of learning something about American jails. He received the license in 1960. Reiner's jobs were over. He had spent about two years on his projects. Now he had to take part in competitive bidding for Eckbo, other architects, and general contractors. This was the start of a whole new chapter in his career.

My parents applied for citizenship within a month of our arrival in Los Angeles and were naturalized five months later in February 1955. Maybe that was when he changed his name. He was born Rafał Feliks Buszejkin, but he died Ralph Felix Bush. I don't remember when we changed our family name, but I also don't remember ever using the name Buszejkin.

I remember my parents' marriage as always being rocky. But it went from bad to worse and finally, after 32 years of marriage, Dad left Mom in 1970, leaving her the house and all our possessions. Like many other parents, mine waited for me to get married.

My mother remarried but later divorced. She had a massive stroke, but, survivor that she was, she fought her way back to speech and limited mobility.

I had spent my teenage years in a socialist-Zionist youth group. My parents weren't Zionists, and I suppose, once I got older, they may have been concerned that I, their only child, would actually pick up and move to Israel. During those years, my father would hire young men from the group, the older counselors, if they needed a job and wanted to do physical labor. So when he got divorced and found himself alone, he headed off to Israel where those young men were now living. But the kibbutz he went to would not accept him as a member. He was too old. I can imagine, after a lifetime of being valued as a professional who knew agriculture and took pride in working with his hands, how disappointing that rejection from an Israeli kibbutz must have been.

In 1972 Dad married Halina Lewandowska. He was embarrassed to tell me and only did so after the fact. In his mind, only the Hollywood stars got divorced and remarried. Halina was a Polish Catholic who had worked in the Polish underground. Her father had been taken hostage at the outset of the German invasion, and her only brother, a soldier in the Polish army, had been killed in the first week of the war. She was 26 when she was arrested by the German secret police in March 1943 and interned as an enemy of the Third Reich. She survived Bergen-Belsen, Ravensbruck, and Neustadt-Gleve. After the war she settled in Belgium where she met her first husband, a Polish Jew. They immigrated to the United States in 1951 and were part of my parents' social circle. They were divorced in 1967.

After Dad and Halina married, they maintained cordial social relations with my mother, and remained an extended family. Halina was not a practicing Catholic, nevertheless, she was proud of Karol Józef Wojtyła, the Polish Pope John Paul II, and had a photograph of him hanging on their wall. Like my mother, Halina was also a seamstress but rather than make clothes for private customers, she worked in Hollywood in the movie industry, making costumes for films like *The King and I*.

Halina had always done drawing and painting, but near the end of her life, when they were living in Thousand Palms, she took a class with the sculptor Kay Henkel and began to sculpt. Once she started there was no stopping. The sculptures came one after another, all memories of her years in the German concentration camps – things she had never talked about. In 1980, after only one year of sculpting, she had a show titled *Memoirs of an Unforgotten Era* with seven of her sculptures at the Aaron Brothers Gallery in Palm Springs.

For a while, they lived and worked on Barbra Streisand's ranch in Malibu Canyon. He took care of the grounds, and she was the housekeeper/cook. But they were already at retirement age and eventually they moved to their house in the mountains. They had bought it a year and a half before and had spent most of their weekends fixing it up. It was located in Running Springs at an elevation of 6,000 feet, between Big Bear and Lake Arrowhead. Halina's health improved in the mountains. She had had lung problems ever since her time working in the concentration camp as a painter. But Dad developed high blood pressure and the doctor advised moving to sea level. So they sold their house and five more lots and moved to Palm Springs where Dad started working again doing maintenance jobs and had a crew of six men.

Halina had an operation for a detached retina followed by Dad having an operation for a hernia. They sold all their real estate, realizing $17,000 and decided it was time to travel. Neither one had traveled in all their years working.

They went to Europe in 1981 for two and a half months visiting Spain, France, Israel, Poland,

and six days in London. While playing tennis in Spain, Dad felt there was something wrong. When they got back, he was diagnosed with Parkinson's. Then one morning Halina woke up at 5:30 feeling very ill. They called an ambulance. It was her first heart attack.

They spent their last years living in a double-wide mobile home in Thousand Palms, in a mobile home park with a country club and golf course. Dad hated golf. It was a long way from all that he had known. But he loved the clean air and the desert landscape. I think it reminded him of Bou Saâda.

His Parkinson's only got worse until Halina could no longer take care of him and he went to live in a nursing home. Halina died on July 16, 1998, and Dad died on March 11, 1999. He was 87. Mom died, two years later, also at the age of 87, on 11 November 2001.They are buried, all three together, at the cemetery in Palm Springs.

Telsa, Luba, Marysia, Dvora, Felek
New York, c. 1950

Coney Island

Driving cross country, 1954

Halina

Marysia

Felek

Afterword

If you've ever read a detective story, you'll know that you never know what you will find once you start digging. I am not a researcher but even still, my amateur digging led to some real treasures.

Often when you look for one thing you find another, perhaps even better than what you were looking for. This happened with a small, 4 ½ by 6 inch clothbound notebook that had once been red. I looked through it once then tucked it away in a drawer for years, where it was safe from dust and forgotten. I noticed it recently, took it out, and took another look.

I remembered that on various pages, it had some drawings. It also had some writing that I couldn't read: a list of some sort with prices in rubles, some names and addresses, and three pages of writing that looked to be in Polish. So I showed my little notebook to the Facebook group Tracing the Tribe, a group that devotes itself to Jewish genealogy.

What I thought might be a shopping list turned out to be just that, listing coal, wood, and a bucket, among other things, and there was a note to get some Abyssinian asthma powder for Lolek.

There were those drawings made with colored pencils, some were by my mother and some by my father. I never knew my father could draw. Each had signed and dated his or her drawing, Dzhambul, February 1943. A couple of them looked like they might have been copied from pictures in a magazine, especially the one my mother drew of Loretta Young.

There was one drawing that was different and stood out. It was of a woman, nicely dressed in European clothes, wearing elegant shoes, and holding a motorcycle with a sidecar. She was talking to a man at the side of the road and was possibly inviting him to come for a ride. They were on a road with one small building and two palm trees behind them – clearly in the desert. It was by my father and looked to be a memory he was invoking of his time in Algiers. At the bottom he had written "*Cielęce lata*" and "*Alger.*" Alger is Algiers in French, but what did the Polish say?

Yale Reisner translated it for me. Cielęce lata means "Calf Years" in Polish and has the same meaning as "Salad Days" in English. In the middle of the war, in far off Kazakhstan, he was remembering what was probably the best time of his youth, when he was in Algeria. In fact, through most of his life, his favorite stories to tell tended to be from his time in Algeria, and it was the California desert where he went to spend his last years.

So they had used the notebook when they were living in Dzhambul and the asthma powder was probably for Lolek Pianko, who they hid and then wrapped in a blanket and put on a train together with their belongings, to ride back to Warsaw after the war.

I hadn't asked about the notebook itself, but someone remarked that the insignia of an eagle on the front cover is the symbol of Poland, and the initials are my father's, last name first.

The writing wasn't Polish, it was Russian, written by my father (who could read, write, and speak Russian since childhood) and turned out to be lyrics to two songs that were popular at that time. One of them is called "Cables" and came from a film called *Twins*. It's a cheerful song, sung by a young woman who is climbing up telephone poles, repairing the cables in a suburban residential neighborhood. A happy proletariat song. The other is called "Accidental Waltz." This is a sad song about a soldier far from home who says:

The night is short
The clouds are asleep
Your unfamiliar hand is lying on my palm
After the troubles
Sleeps the little town
I heard the melody of the waltz
And stopped here for a little while

Though I don't know you at all
And far from here is my home
I feel as though
I am home again
In this empty room,
We dance together,
So say something...
I don't know what

Several members of the group posted various performances of those two songs, including a clip from the original *Twins* movie, all of them on YouTube.

Probably the most serendipitous discovery resulted from my question on 7 October 2023 to the same group about Solomon Pelix who my father wrote about twice: once when he came to visit the family in Warsaw in the late 1920s, and later, in 1946, when my parents went to Nice to wait for their visas and my father went to work for Solomon, delivering orange marmalades.

My father had written that one of his mother's aunts had married a man by the name of Felix. This man owned one of the biggest forest plantations in the region (he didn't say what region) and had two sons. The two sons were sent to study in Switzerland; he never says the name of the older son, but the younger one was named Solomon. But later he refers to him as Solomon Pelix. One or the other was a typing error. But which one? Felix or Pelix?

When the Russian Revolution broke out, father Feliz/Pelix was killed, supposedly by his workers, and Solomon left Switzerland and went to France.

My post did not yield any useful replies until five weeks later when someone in the group responded about a postcard they had seen on EBay. It was written by a Chaim Pelix to his son Solomon in Switzerland in 1914. This was Greg Livshitz, a group member, genealogist, and Judaica post card collector who wrote "Dvora, this is a 1914 post card addressed to Solomon Pelix in Switzerland from Ch. Pelix in Minsk." Accompanying the message was an image of the postcard with a link to EBay.

The postcard was written in Russian and I asked Greg if he could possibly translate it? Yes, he could:

"Dear Solomon, we haven't received any letter from you in a long time, today we are delighted with Firochka's letter, and she didn't write anything about you. I sent money to Yakov and you will receive it from him, but transferring money now is difficult and I really don't know how you will live on our money with the current exchange rate. Yakov probably earns a little, but it's probably more difficult for you to find a job. We have nothing new, I wrote in detail to Yakov. Try to do something because the time will come when only ??? people will be able to exist. God grant that you can come home and get settled. My work in Priluki is ending soon and they are offering me to move the plant to another place, but I don't know if I'll do it again and it's difficult to earn anything with this ??? I look forward to your letters. Your father kisses you, Ch, Pelix."

So, their name was Pelix, Solomon's older brother was named Jacob, and he also had a sister called Firochka.

I signed up on EBay and tried to buy the postcard, but a few minutes after I signed up I was suspended with no reason given. The suspension wasn't temporary, it was permanent, for life they said, and if I tried to change my name they would still know it was me and God knows what they would do then.

Next, Greg wrote that the postcard hadn't sold yet and I could buy it if I liked, and I explained my situation with regard to EBay. Greg offered to buy the postcard for me and have it shipped directly to me, and I could reimburse him. We did that.

The same day that we made the arrangements for the postcard, Greg wrote to me asking if I had seen a biography on the internet and sent me a link. It was to an article about Jakob Pelix, Solomon's older brother, written by his nephew and published (in English) on the internet on what I believe is a Polish website called Centropa. Although it gave one conflicting piece of information, it also provided a lot of interest. You never know what will turn up when you ask questions of a group of genealogists.

The postcard arrived in the mail from the German EBay seller a couple of weeks later. There is something absolutely thrilling to come upon a family memento by chance and end up being able to actually hold it in your hands.

Ed Mitukiewicz, also at Tracing the Tribe, helped me find information about Leopold Infeld who, Dad said, when he mentioned how distinguished some of the faculty was, had taught physics at his high school. Infield did indeed teach at a Warsaw high school from 1924 to 1930 when he finally got an academic appointment in Lwów (now Lviv), and eventually he went to Princeton where he collaborated with Albert Einstein during 1936-1938. Ed also managed to find a page from the 1938-39 Warsaw telephone directory listing my grandfather at their address at Lezno 56. Seeing a photocopy of a page like that can be a wonderful surprise and quite a shock. My father mentions that address many times in his memoir. It was where my mother's family and the Kozłowskis came to stay after the early bombing of Warsaw. Ed also found a photo of that building, taken in 1939 before it was destroyed by the Nazis, on the Fundacja Warszawa 1939 website.

I came across the name of the hotel where the Joint set us up in New York by chance when I was reading an article by Joseph Berger about immigration in the New York Times and he mentioned that he and his family stayed in lodgings provided by an aid society on 87th and Amsterdam Avenue. My father had written that we stayed in a hotel provided by the Joint on 87th and Broadway. It turned out they were one and the same place called Capitol Hall, on 87th between Broadway and Amsterdam Avenue.

Someone suggested I should explain that the Kazakhs and other Central Asian groups like the Chechens were mostly Muslim. I thought about adding something, but decided not to. Surely he knew, but he never mentioned it. Such things didn't concern him. He noted that people were honest or corrupt, strong, good sportsmen, or hard-working. He described what interested him about their culture. Those were the things he cared about, and I didn't want to change that.

Finally, I was struck by my father's friendships, how deep and long-lasting they were. In an era that predated the internet, he and his friends managed to find each other and stayed in touch. There would be onionskin letters in lightweight blue Par Avion envelopes coming and going, or aerograms, or the occasional long distance phone call. People came to visit us from New York, Israel, and Australia. He somehow found Georges in Paris, Bruce in California, Helenka in Australia. Once reunited, they all wrote letters to each other and stayed in touch until the end of their lives.

The Red Polish Notebook

Salad Days

Chaim Pelix postcard

Acknowledgements

I am truly grateful to Sophie Rosenberg and Carol Nechemias who generously agreed to read a late draft and who gave me invaluable comments and suggestions for improvements.

Sincere thanks to Greg Livshitz and Ed Mitukiewicz, from Tracing the Tribe, two people I have never even met who helped me discover several small treasures. Greg Livshitz in particular went beyond the call of duty to help me obtain that incredible postcard from 1914.

Yale Reisner, also from Tracing the Tribe, gave generously of his time to do several translations, most notably the "Salad Days" caption on that wonderful, nostalgic drawing of my father's. Short as that was, it turned a sweet drawing into a meaningful memento.

My father was not a writer. But one day, when he was 64 years old, he sat down to write his stories. He wrote by hand for three years and for the next 14 years, on and off, he had sections typed by various typists. This was a labor of love. He went to all that trouble because he wanted me to know. Without that labor of love, I would know much less about his life and the world he came from, and there would be no book.

Rafał Feliks Buszejkin
Born: 30 January 1912
Ralph Felix Bush
Died: 11 March 1999

Milton Keynes UK
Ingram Content Group UK Ltd.
UKHW041902180724
445674UK00004B/165